Library of
Davidson College

JOHNNY BELINDA

BY ELMER HARRIS

DRAMATISTS
PLAY SERVICE
INC.

JOHNNY BELINDA
Copyright © Renewed 1967, Victor Harris and Blaney Harris
Copyright © 1940, Elmer Harris

All Rights Reserved

CAUTION: Professionals and amateurs are hereby warned that performance of JOHNNY BELINDA is subject to payment of a royalty. It is fully protected under the copyright laws of the United States of America, and of all countries covered by the International Copyright Union (including the Dominion of Canada and the rest of the British Commonwealth), and of all countries covered by the Pan-American Copyright Convention, the Universal Copyright Convention, the Berne Convention, and of all countries with which the United States has reciprocal copyright relations. All rights, including professional/amateur stage rights, motion picture, recitation, lecturing, public reading, radio broadcasting, television, video or sound recording, all other forms of mechanical or electronic reproduction, such as CD-ROM, CD-I, DVD, information storage and retrieval systems and photocopying, and the rights of translation into foreign languages, are strictly reserved. Particular emphasis is placed upon the matter of readings, permission for which must be secured from the Author's agent in writing.

The English language amateur stage performance rights in the United States, its territories, possessions and Canada for JOHNNY BELINDA are controlled exclusively by DRAMATISTS PLAY SERVICE, INC., 440 Park Avenue South, New York, NY 10016. No nonprofessional performance of the Play may be given without obtaining in advance the written permission of DRAMATISTS PLAY SERVICE, INC., and paying the requisite fee.

Inquiries concerning all other rights should be addressed to Dramatists Play Service, Inc., 440 Park Avenue South, New York, NY 10016.

SPECIAL NOTE

Anyone receiving permission to produce JOHNNY BELINDA is required to give credit to the Author as sole and exclusive Author of the Play on the title page of all programs distributed in connection with performances of the Play and in all instances in which the title of the Play appears for purposes of advertising, publicizing or otherwise exploiting the Play and/or a production thereof. The name of the Author must appear on a separate line, in which no other name appears, immediately beneath the title and in size of type equal to 50% of the size of the largest, most prominent letter used for the title of the Play. No person, firm or entity may receive credit larger or more prominent than that accorded the Author.

THE LORD'S PRAYER

Demonstrating the use of the Deaf Mute Sign Language

IMPORTANT NOTICE

The author believes strongly that production groups undertaking JOHNNY BELINDA should familiarize themselves with the deaf mute sign language invented by the eighteenth century French priest and teacher, the Abbe de l'Epee. These are "visual signs," which suggest the things talked about, and which have such beauty and ballet-like grace that their meaning is readily conveyed to the audience. Their use will draw audiences more deeply into the play, and heighten their sympathy, understanding and enjoyment of it.

The accompanying plates show "The Lord's Prayer" signed in this manner, and we gratefully acknowledge the permission granted by Gallaudet College to reproduce them. Gallaudet, which is the only college in the United States devoted exclusively to deaf persons, has also indicated its willingness to assist producing groups in other ways as well. Copies of "The Sign Language" by J. Schuyler Long may be secured from Gallaudet at a price of $4.00 each, plus postage, and we add that this book, with its photographs and lucid descriptions, is of incalculable value for production purposes. Gallaudet has also agreed to supply, on request, information regarding the locations of schools and teachers for the deaf who would be willing to assist in "on the spot" preparation and coaching. We believe that having such expert assistance would prove invaluable, and we urge that this generous offer be acted on.

Please address all inquiries for such information to:
> Gallaudet College
> Kendall Green, N.E.
> Washington 2, D.C.

FOREWORD

The time of the play is the year 1900.

The scene of the play is an island, south of Newfoundland and northwest of Nova Scotia, jutting out into the mystery of the Atlantic, and known among the Maritime Provinces of Canada as the garden spot of the Gulf. It is a garden spot during only a few months of the year, for the snow still lingers under the pines at the end of May, and frost turns the maples to scarlet, and the silver birches to gold in late September; but during this short summer nature unshoulders her cornucopia of abundance.

The capital, besides its ample harbor, boasts of a stone cathedral with twin spires, the Governor's mansion tucked away in a grove of birch, a city park with courthouse and public market, and about four square blocks of paved streets, teeming with farm wagons on the market days. For the most part, the houses are of weather-beaten shingle, with tall peaked roofs to shed the winter weight of snow. A one-track railroad serves the length and breadth of the Island; and in the outlying districts lives a hard-bitten race of farmers, who divide their time between fishing and tilling a stubborn soil.

The play is laid at the eastern end of the island in a bleak little village perched on a cliff with a winding road down to the wharves where the cod fishermen put in, and where the cod are gutted and salted before being dried on stave tables along the cliffs.

The lobster fishing, with canneries at various harbors which fringe the coast, begins in May and lasts for eight weeks, the farmers with their boats tending about a hundred traps each, selling their catch at the local factory. Each farmer has his pigs, sheep, geese, and cattle, the whole family sharing in the labor of the farm, from the grandmother who spins and works at her loom, to the children who help with the chores. Rail fences must be repaired, barns shingled, and barn doors painted the customary brick-red, the more prosperous of the farmers white-washing their houses every year or two. The soil, while fertile, has been worked for many generations, and requires nursing. It is done in a primitive way. In winter oyster shells are dredged from the river beds, and thrown on the land for lime every five years as crops are rotated from potatoes to hay. The Island is beset by furious summer storms. As skies clear, red-wheeled, one-horse carts may be seen winding down to the shore, where each farmer gathers his share of kelp, which is used as fertilizer.

Once the fishing is over, the crops planted, these Scotch-Irish farmers, with a sprinkling of French, can relax in such diversions as the Sunday-school picnic, with rustic arbors built in the fields, or a dance at the Schoolhouse, the local fiddler supplying tunes inherited from father to son on an instrument which has never been properly tuned; old and young join in square dances, the fiddler tapping his heel in time with his music. More important is the Fair at the Capital, where farmers exhibit their prize stock, stand in awe at the six-legged calf, and risk a few odd dollars on the trotting races.

Of course, now, half a century later, with automobiles and radios the prized possessions of farmers who can, or cannot, afford them, times have somewhat changed; but only a few years back the country people still wore homespun, and tumbledown mills ground their grain or buckwheat. A highly religious comunity still, where church-going is all but compulsory, and where descration of the Sabbath can mean jail.

This is the background of the play.

CAST OF CHARACTERS

Policeman
Hector McGuffey
Mrs. Lutz
Dr. Jack Davidson
Floyd McGuiggan
Jimmy Dingwell
Fergus McGuiggan
Mrs. McKee
Locky McCormick
Stella Maguire
Pacquet
Belinda McDonald
Black McDonald
Andy McPhearson
Lizzie Gordon
Maggie McDonald
Reverend Tidmarsh
Defense Counsel McVail
Attorney General McKnight
The Judge
Clerk of the Court
Matron

SYNOPSIS OF SCENES

ACT ONE
Scene 1: A street in the village.
Scene 2: A grist mill.
Scene 3: The same.

ACT TWO
Scene 1: Black McDonald's kitchen.
Scene 2: The same.
Scene 3: A bedroom.
Scene 4: The kitchen.

ACT THREE
Scene 1: The kitchen.
Scene 2: The same.
Scene 3: The courtroom.

JOHNNY BELINDA

ACT ONE

Scene 1

A painted drop shows the harbor of a little fishing village, with the masts of the fishing smacks, a lighthouse in the distance and along the cliffs a row of cottages. On stage left, is the entrance to that of Dr. Davidson's cottage, which serves as his home and office.

As curtain rises, a Policeman enters from L. and crosses McGuffey who enters from R. McGuffey carries a big codfish, his fingers through the gills, the tail dragging.

POLICEMAN. Good day, McGuffey, how's the catch?
McGUFFEY. Pretty fair! Takin' one home fer dinner. (*Both exit, crossing to opposite sides of stage. Mrs. Lutz enters, R. followed by Dr. Jack from his house.*)
DR. JACK. It's a nice day, Mrs. Lutz.
MRS. LUTZ. It is that, Doctor. Will you be giving me any medicine?
DR. JACK. No, Mrs. Lutz. Have your teeth examined.
MRS. LUTZ. The dentist said he'd pull all my teeth and fix me up a set with a gold one in front to make me look natural.
DR. JACK. Don't have all your teeth pulled yet. Have the dentist give them a good going over. I want to see if your teeth are causing your backache.
MRS. LUTZ. And you'd really be able to tell that? My, but you're a smart man! (*Floyd runs in from L.*)
FLOYD. Oh, excuse me, sir! Are you the new Doctor?
DR. JACK. I am.
FLOYD. Could you be sewing on a thumb?
DR. JACK. Whose thumb?

FLOYD. Jimmy Dingwell's. He was helpin' us corn some beef and the cleaver slipped and chopped off the tip of his thumb!
DR. JACK. Where is he?
FLOYD. Out in the rig. He was fixin' to drive to town to Dr. McLaughlin.
DR. JACK. That's sixteen miles! You'd better fetch him in here.
FLOYD. I will, sir! (*He runs off* L.)
DR. JACK. Who's that, Mrs. Lutz?
MRS. LUTZ. (*She goes up steps to watch Floyd run after Jimmy.*) One of the McGuiggan byes. Nice enough lads durin' the day whin they're hard at work, but terrors at night the way they chase the girls. That'd be Floyd, I'm thinkin'.
DR. JACK. And who's Jimmy Dingwell?
MRS. LUTZ. Oh, he's a character around town. Butchers a cow now an' then an' peddles it to the farmers. (*Dingwell enters from* L. *with Fergus holding his right arm.*)
DINGWELL. Doctor, I lost the tip of me thumb. Me eyesight must be gettin' bad. (*Dr. Jack examines thumb.*)
FERGUS. 'Twas our fault, Jimmy, an' we're terrible sorry aboot it.
DINGWELL. Nay, lad, don't be upset, but I'll have to learn ye to use the cleaver.
DR. JACK. Take him into the house, Floyd!
FERGUS. I'm not Floyd, sir, I'm Fergus! (*Fergus and Dingwell exit into Doctor's house. Floyd runs in with tomato can from* L.)
FLOYD. I'm Floyd, sir! (*Offering the tomato can.*) And here's the tip of Jimmy's thumb. Think you kin sew it back on?
DR. JACK. We'll see. Take it into the office. (*Floyd exits into Doctor's house.*) Excuse me, please.
MRS. LUTZ. Why yes, of course, doctor. (*Dr. Jack exits into house. Mrs. McKee enters,* L.)
MRS. McKEE. Well, Mrs. Lutz. You're aboot early!
MRS. LUTZ. Oh, Mrs. McKee, good day, dear!
MRS. McKEE. What are you doin' here, Mrs. Lutz?
MRS. LUTZ. Just consultin' the doctor aboot me backache. He suspects 'tis me teeth.
MRS. McKEE. Teeth! And what have teeth to do with a backache? I think it disgraceful the way you middle-aged women are flockin' around this young doctor. Why don't you go to Dr. McLaughlin, a man o' yer own age an' a church mimber at that.
MRS. LUTZ. I been to 'im, and he done me no good!

MRS. McKEE. Ye'll get no good from this man with his new-fangled ideas. Look what he done to Mrs. Johnny John John.
MRS. LUTZ. I know, sent her to town to have her arteries cut out!
MRS. McKEE. Not arteries, Mrs. Lutz. (*Whispers.*)
MRS. LUTZ. Oh, that's what they call them! Well, anyway, I went in to see her yesterday and she says she feels ten years younger.
MRS. McKEE. She may feel younger layin' there in bed. But wait till she gits up and tries to do her housework. She'll fall apart.
MRS. LUTZ. She never was much for housework, with all of her pains and aches.
MRS. McKEE. Her house is a pig-pen. I'm on me way to see her now. She needs help, poor thing. I'm takin' it up with the Ladies' Aid.
MRS. LUTZ. Give Mrs. Johnny John John my sympathy.
MRS. McKEE. I will, dear, but it's not your sympathy nor mine she appreciates. She's all the time ravin' aboot "that handsome young doctor," and her sixty-five! Bewitched she is! So watch yourself with him, Mrs. Lutz. (*Rev. Tidmarsh enters from* L.) Oh, good day, Mr. Tidmarsh!
MRS. LUTZ. Good day, yer Riverence!
TIDMARSH. Good day, Ladies!
MRS. McKEE. What brings you down to this part of the village?
TIDMARSH. I'm on me way to John McGuffey's. (*Mrs. McKee turns her back at the mention of McGuffey.*) He's a godless man himself, but his wife's a good church mimber and an excellent cook. Last night she made another contribution to the human race.
MRS. McKEE. Yes, that woman done it again? She must have a baker's dozen!
TIDMARSH. 'Tis her fourteenth, Mrs. McKee.
MRS. LUTZ. Fourteen brats an' her husband's lucky if he gets one day's work a month!
MRS. McKEE. Fourteen children! Wonder the man has time to do a day's work!
TIDMARSH. We must be charitable, Mrs. McKee. St. Paul says " 'Tis better to marry than to burn," and Lizzy McGuffey is a dutiful wife. Moreover she always bakes a fine batch of cookies before goin' into labor, which makes visitin' her a special pleasure. Well, I'll see you both at the Ladies' Aid on Thursday.
MRS. McKEE. Yes, indeed, Mr. Tidmarsh.
MRS. LUTZ. Good day, yer Riverence.

TIDMARSH. Good day, ladies. (*He exits* R.)
MRS. McKEE. Huh! The reverend can quote St. Paul to kiver up licentiousness, but if you ask me, it's the book of Genesis that's responsible for settin' the pace—with all those "begets and begats." There are parts of the scriptures that shouldn't be read in public when you're strivin' to stamp out sin.
MRS. LUTZ. You can't call it sin, when a man's married!
MRS. McKEE. It's the original sin, Mrs. Lutz. The weakness of the Flesh, the fourteen children don't excuse it. They're just an indication of what's really takin' place. (*Locky enters* R.)
MRS. LUTZ. Ah, Locky, me lad! How's the lobster fishin'?
LOCKY. Not too bad, Mrs. Lutz, four hundred pounds this morning.
MRS. LUTZ. A fine catch!
LOCKY. 'Tain't always as good, though. The season's only eight weeks an' you can't make any real money when you have to sell all yer lobsters to that old storekeeper Pocket!
MRS. LUTZ. Don't he pay you good?
LOCKY. Good! Four cents a pound, that's all he'll give. I'm goin' to have it out with that pot-bellied Mic-Mac and damn soon, too!
MRS. LUTZ. Careful now, Locky. He's the only man rich enough to wear a white collar durin' the week an' live in a three-story house.
LOCKY. That don't scare me none! (*Stella enters from the doctor's door to shake a rug, a hooked mat.*)
MRS. LUTZ. Ah! Good day, Stella!
STELLA. Good day, Mrs. Lutz, Mrs. McKee. Hello, Locky!
LOCKY. Kinda late on yer new job, ain't ye?
STELLLA. I was here at eight o'clock. The doctor sent me to Pocket's store for some flies. He's goin' fishin'.
MRS. McKEE. That's all the man does. Last Sunday he was fishin' at Grand River when the carriages was goin' to church. A fine example to be settin' the young men o' the sittlement! (*Stella, annoyed, shakes rug in Mrs. McKee's face. Mrs. McKee sneezes and gags.*) Stella! Are ye tryin' to choke me? Hang it on the line an' give it a beatin'. (*Stella pays no attention.*) I'm sorry to see ye workin' fer that man, Stella.
STELLA. (*Indignant.*) He's a fine doctor, Mrs. McKee. He's a Psy-Ky-a somethin' ye can't even pronounce.

MRS. McKEE. Probably somethin' not fit to mention! Well, I'm off to the store. (*She exits,* R.)

STELLA. Are ye takin' me to the dance Saturday, Locky?

LOCKY. You know I'm not strong fer dances. (*Moving to her.*)

STELLA. But ye promised!

LOCKY. I'll see!

STELLA. There's goin' to be a jig contest! (*She exits into Doctor's house with the rug.*)

MRS. LUTZ. Do ye think you'll marry Stella, Locky?

LOCKY. She's sure hot fer it. (*Sitting on the steps of the Doctor's house.*)

MRS. LUTZ. You could do worse. Stella'll bring ye a farm of two hundred acres. Not every girl can do that.

LOCKY. That old Aitken farm her uncle left? That's all run out. Ain't been farmed since he died. Must be three years now.

MRS. LUTZ. A few loads of kelp an' some oyster shells will fetch it back in heart. And there's a fine stand o' spruce on the back field, enough to build ye a new house and wood aplenty to keep ye warm fer many's the winter. You'd be rich, Locky, worth thinkin' aboot.

LOCKY. No hurry!

MRS. LUTZ. Lord knows your own family ain't got any too much. Be one way o' helpin' yer father out.

LOCKY. Stella's all right, Mrs. Lutz. Though she ain't what ye'd call a beauty!

MRS. LUTZ. 'Tain't the beauties that make the best wives, me lad!

LOCKY. No, but it helps a hell of a lot, if you know what I mean.

MRS. LUTZ. (*Shocked.*) Oh, Locky! (*She exits* L. *Pacquet enters* R.)

PACQUET. Ah! McCormick! Vous voila! I look for you!

LOCKY. Well, what do you want, Pocket?

PACQUET. Aujourdhui, one half the lobsters you land comme ca, undersize, like shrimp.

LOCKY. At four cents a pound I can't be bothered sortin' them. I'd starve to death.

PACQUET. If the inspector see them, I am fine five hundred dollars.

LOCKY. Boost the price and I'll toss back the little ones.

PACQUET. My price!—Four cents. C'est magnifique!

LOCKY. Ashley at Southport pays six!

PACQUET. Well, then, go to Southport. Allez vous en! (*Locky rises, follows Pacquet.*)

LOCKY. Drive thirty miles a day and back? I'd be givin' the two extra cents to the blacksmith or the veterinary. And while we're talkin' aboot it, ye dammed ol' skinflint ——

PACQUET. Comment!

LOCKY. Don't get yer hackles up, Frenchy! Not with that tub o' guts, ye'd not last two rounds. (*He threatens to punch Pacquet in stomach.*) It's aboot time someone took ye down a peg. Ye sell yer lobsters to the same cannery as Ashley an' get the same fancy prices and knock down two cents the pound on us farmers.

PACQUET. Les affaires sont les affaires!

LOCKY. What's that, Mic-Mac Indian?

PACQUET. Comment!

LOCKY. Yer a half-breed an' ye know it!

PACQUET. Ecoutez! Jeune homme! Tomorrow you do not fish that reef! Another man not you will fish that reef. (*He turns to go, but Locky turns him around and grabs him by coat lapels.*)

LOCKY. Oh, he will, will he? I've fished that reef for ten years. You let anyone touch that line of traps and by the Godfrey, I'll drown him in two fathoms of water! (*Releases Pacquet.*)

PACQUET. Nous avons maintenant, mon vieux, les homme de police!

LOCKY. To hell with the Police! Tis the law of the sea, first come, first served. Ye kape yer crew off that reef!

PACQUET. Nous allons voir, mon vieux, nous allons voir! Et maintenant, Mr. Locky McCormick. You owe big bill at my store. You know that, eh? Yesterday your father with tears in his eye ask me to extend his note. I do not extend it! No more favors! You pay or I take your stinky farm. No one, not even Locky McCormick, can insult Sevier Pacquet. Mic-Mac Indian, eh? Well, you pay me. You pay me tomorrow. Tell your father that, Mr. Locky McCormick! (*He exits* L.)

LOCKY. Why, you greasy old half-breed! Try and take that farm and I'll gut you out like a cod. (*Locky starts off* R. *then hesitates, glancing towards the doctor's house, wherein is Stella. After another glance at the retreating Pacquet, he comes back and calls in through window.*) Stella!

STELLA. (*Within.*) Yes, Locky.

LOCKY. Come here a shake.
STELLA. All right. (*Stella enters from house.*) What is it, Locky?
LOCKY. What dress are you wearin' to the dance Saturday night—the one I like?
STELLA. Why, yes. Then you are goin' to take me?
LOCKY. Of course I am.
STELLA. Oh, I'm so excited.
LOCKY. (*With his hands on Stella's waist.*) I been thinkin' things over, Stella. We ought to git married, and the sooner the better.
STELLA. Oh, Locky, I'll make ye such a good wife!
LOCKY. Then it's a bargain?
STELLA. Of course it is! Oh, I think I'm goin' to cry!
LOCKY. Aw! Blow yer nose, and don't look so silly!
STELLA. I can't help it! I'm so happy!
LOCKY. I'll pick you up early for the dance, so I can stop by the mill and git me flour.
STELLA. I'll be ready.
LOCKY. Oh—Stella——Tell me this: yer uncle's farm—are ye sure yer old man will give it to ye?
STELLA. 'Tis mine already. The deeds were signed last week.
LOCKY. That's great!
STELLA. We'll make a go of it, Locky. Sakes! How I've planned for it! We'll build a house facin' the river, and the children can play on the beach.
LOCKY. The children? By the Godfrey, ye are countin' yer chickens before they're hatched!
STELLA. Oh! Locky! (*She kisses him. Floyd and Fergus enter from the Doctor's house, followed by Dingwell who is a little unsteady on his feet. Dr. Jack follows them on. He wears his rubber boots, waders, up to his hips. Stella slips past them into house.*)
DR. JACK. Come in Saturday for a dressing, Mr. Dingwell.
DINGWELL. I will, Doctor. (*Staggers.*) Ooops!
LOCKY. What's the matter with him?
FERGUS. Got the end of his thumb cut off.
DR. JACK. (*Calling back.*) Bring Mr. Dingwell the whiskey, Stella.
LOCKY. Guess this'll kind of put ye out of business, Dingwell?
DINGWELL. Don't ye believe it. There's that white cow of Johnny Arthur's. He's had her to the bull three times but she

didn't catch. If he'll sell her, I'll be butchering her next week, thumb or no thumb.

LOCKY. Save us the brisket.

DINGWELL. 'Tis yers, Locky. (*Stella enters with whiskey, and pours drink for him.*)

FLOYD. Locky, if ye ain't takin' Stella to the dance Saturday, I'd like to.

FERGUS. I put in for her first.

FLOYD. Her an' I've practiced a step for the contest.

FERGUS. Her'n I've got one, too.

LOCKY. Wait a minute, byes, I'm takin' her. For your information, I'm goin' to marry her. I'll be around tonight, Stella.

STELLA. I'll expect you. (*She waves to him and he exits,* L., *with Floyd and Fergus who slap him on the back and congratulate him.*)

DINGWELL. A bit of advice, me girl—if yer fixin' to marry Locky—from the way the females behave at the lobster factory, every time his boat sails in, you'd best put him on ice!

STELLA. I think I kin manage him, Mr. Dingwell. I'll get yer rod and creel, Doctor. (*She exits into Doctor's house* L.)

DINGWELL. About yer bill, Doctor——

DR. JACK. I'll leave that up to you.

DINGWELL. Jimmy Burke says he give ye a couple of brass candlesticks fer gittin' the fish bone out of his bye's gullet.

DR. JACK. Yes, I took the candlesticks.

DINGWELL. I'll drop by and leave ye a bit of beef.

DR. JACK. That'll be fine. (*Stella returns with rod and creel. Mrs. McKee returns* R. *with some bundles in her arms—she's been to the store.*)

STELLA. Here are yer things, Doctor.

DR. JACK. Thank you, Stella. (*Stella exits into house.*)

DINGWELL. So yer a fisherman, be ye? (*Pouring himself another drink.*)

DR. JACK. There don't seem to be many other diversions around here, that I can find.

MRS. McKEE. There seems to be plenty of liquor.

DINGWELL. Would ye be grudgin' a drop to a man who's just lost his arm?

MRS. McKEE. Dr. McLaughlin is able to cure a little ache without makin' the patient unconscious.

DINGWELL. A little ache! Did ye ever lose the tip of anything?

MRS. McKEE. I never knew a man yit who could stand a mite o' pain.
DR. JACK. Mr. Dingwell. I haven't met Mrs. McKee. (*Moving to Dingwell.*)
DINGWELL. Well, don't go lookin' fer trouble.
MRS. McKEE. You insulting old man! And if yer lookin' to Jimmy Dingwell fer social introductions, Dr. Davidson, I'm afraid you won't git very far in this village. (*She exits* L.)
DR. JACK. What are you trying to do, Mr. Dingwell, put me in bad standing with the first lady of this comunity?
DINGWELL. (*Rising and moving* L. *a few steps.*) That ould hypocrite!—With her airs and graces! (*Dr. Jack sits on the steps, fastens a leader to the end of his line, then selecting flies from his fly-book, puts two flies on the leader and reels in the line.*) Twenty-five years ago she tried to be the Town Flirt—and no man'd have her account of that face! Then Johnny McKee got up the courage to seduce her. He told me later 'twas nae worth the effort. (*He reaches behind Dr. Jack for bottle and refills his glass, replacing bottle.*) But she hooked him—made him marry her—then nagged him into an early grave. Well, sir, she couldn't land another man, so she's turned religious, teamed up with ould Tidmarsh here, with his Hell and Damnation, and goes around town chasin' sin with a broomstick—Whackin' its head whenever she sees it.
DR. JACK. I don't see much sin around, Mr. Dingwell. Seems like a very moral community.
DINGWELL. It is. Of course there's the usual diversions that young people go in fer—when they're bent on the business of Cupid. You can notice it on a moonlight night.
DR. JACK. I have yet to hear of any scandal.
DINGWELL. And for good reason. If a bye gits a girl in trouble he marries her, for 'tis the Law if he don't he must pay the Father seven hundred and fifty dollars for support of the brat, or go to jail for a nice long stay.
DR. JACK. I see.
DINGWELL. Apart from that, man dear, children are welcome. Without sons to help on these farms here, a man can starve to death. So the young folks have their fun, and it all works out for the gineral good.
DR. JACK. A very practical arrangement, at any rate.

DINGWELL. Where do you go ter your troot, Doctor? (*He places glass on steps.*)
DR. JACK. Thought I'd try Black Pond today. Never been there, but I've heard about it.
DINGWELL. Ah! Look out fer Black McDonald. He owns the Grist mill there, a harsh unfriendly man, sir. He'll fight if you look sideways at him. A terrible timper he has!
DR. JACK. He won't fight me if I try to fish in his pond, will he? (*Slinging on his creel.*)
DINGWELL. Best ask him first. He's terrible touchy. A proud man he is, sir—a direct descendent of the original settler—the first John McDonald—a man much respected at the Court of George the Third.
DR. JACK. He sounds like an interesting character, Mr. Dingwell.
DINGWELL. Ah! He's all of that. Of course the Widow McKee will tell ye, "He ain't been to church these fifteen years." Ye know why? He had the sweetest wife God ever let live—come over she did from Scotland. Oh, and a beauty. Well, she died, and Black McDonald—a good church mimber, mind ye,—wanted to sit by the windy where he could see his wife's grave, and Charley Coffin wouldn't give up the pew. "To hell with ye," says Black McDonald. He ain't been to church since—and 'tis few—in the sittlement he'll hold traffic with.
DR. JACK. Well, thanks for the advice, Mr. Dingwell. Drop in Saturday so I can dress your thumb—we'll have a pipe together.
DINGWELL. Thank you, Doctor. (*Stella returns.*)
DR. JACK. I'll be back for dinner, Stella.
STELLA. It'll be ready, Doctor. (*Dr. Jack exits with creel and rod L.*)
DINGWELL. A right nice young man, Stella. (*Stella picks up the tray with bottle and glass.*)
STELLA. Oh, and a gintleman, Mr. Dingwell, from Muntreal.
DINGWELL. I'm glad to find ye here, Stella, earnin' an honest dollar. 'Tis better than gaddin' aboot.
STELLA. I'm savin' up fer me trousseau, Mr. Dingwell, I've got a catalogue. They got the most beautiful things in all colors.
DINGWELL. Then 'tis all set between you and Locky?
STELLA. Yes, Mr. Dingwell—we're promised.
DINGWELL. Well, me girl, I'd like to congratulate you, fer this

should be the happiest time o' yer life; but as Locky's wife—ye'll have a lot o' competition. Ye'll have to be in bed early to hold him. (*He exits L. as:*)

CURTAIN COMES DOWN

ACT ONE

Scene 2

Black McDonald's Grist Mill.
Through an open double door at the back left may be seen the mill pond and the trees around it. Left, a pile of sacks full of grain. Right, the hopper into which the grain is poured when being ground, a lever turning it on and off. An old harness and horse collars hang on a peg, a coil of rope hangs on another, a fish net is draped over a couple of other pegs. Hoes, shovels, rakes, a pickax stand piled in a corner. The grist mill is a bit of a storeroom as well as a flour mill.
Belinda, barefoot, in a ragged dress, her tousled hair falling to her shoulders, is discovered scooping grain from a a sack into the hopper. She lifts the nearly empty sack and dumps all the grain from it into the hopper, shaking out the bag as Dr. Jack appears in the open doorway with rod and creel.

DR. JACK. Do you mind if I throw a line in the mill pond? (*He gets no answer, so he goes down nearer the girl.*) Would you mind if I threw —— (*Belinda turns and is startled at seeing him.*) Oh, forgive me for startling you. I just wanted to know if I could fish here. (*Belinda notices his rod and creel, crosses to the door, takes the bell and stepping outside, rings it vigorously. Then, replacing the bell on the broken chair, she goes to the pile of sacks and starts to lift one. Dr. Jack hurries toward her.*) Here, let me lift that for you. (*Belinda, not hearing him, pays no attention, lifts the sack and carries it to the hopper where she opens it with a knife. Black McDonald appears in the open doorway.*)
McDONALD. Well?
DR. JACK. Oh—good afternoon. You must be Black McDonald. (*Moving up toward doorway.*)

McDONALD. I be.

DR. JACK. Would you mind if I took a few trout from the mill pond? I saw them jumping out there.

McDONALD. It'll cost ye fifty cents. (*Dr. Jack taking coins from his pocket.*)

DR. JACK. I'm the new doctor in the village.

McDONALD. Oh! Then it'll cost ye twenty-five (*McDonald takes a quarter. Dr. Jack returns other quarter to his pocket.*)

DR. JACK. Oh, thanks. I asked the young lady if I might fish, but got little satisfaction.

McDONALD. Oh—me daughter—she's deef and dumb.

DR. JACK. Deaf and dumb! Why that's terrible.

McDONALD. What she don't know, don't hurt her none.

DR. JACK. Was she born deaf?

McDONALD. Nay. She was took down with a faver when aboot a year old. An' when it come time to talk—as babies will—no sound come from her. An' she growed up that way—dumb.

DR. JACK. Has she ever been to school?

McDONALD. School? Man dear, she's deef and dumb. There's no larnin' her nothin'. All she knows is what I bate into her. (*He takes a small cheap notebook hanging with its pencil from a nail, and shows the pages to the Doctor.*) Here's the extint of her larnin'. I put a symbol at the top of a page for each customer— a cross fer McGinnis, a circle for McGuffey, two parallel lines for the Mc-Guiggans and so forth, an' headin's fer buckwheat or oats or wheat —flour, an' as the sacks come in, the dummy marks 'em down, an' whin they're ground she marks 'em off. See fer yourself, man. She's larned to identify each man by his mark—an' I will say this: She niver makes a mistake. (*He hangs book up again.*)

DR. JACK. That shows, Mr. McDonald, your daughter's an intelligent girl, and if you'd send her to a school for the deaf —— There's a good one in Montreal. I attended the pupils there while studying medicine ——

McDONALD. Muntreal! That costs money—and money don't grow on trees in Kings County. We're lucky to kape body and soul togither, we farmers.

DR. JACK. I know but —— (*He glances at Belinda.*) She could be taught; I'm sure of it.

McDONALD. (*He becomes interested.*) Well now, the doctor ahead iv ye said she feels things. Tho' what she feels the Almighty only knows. She seems to be fond of colors. All them flowers out there be hers. And years ago whin I took her to church oncet and they took and played the organ, a look came on her face like she heard, but I knew she nay could hear a sound. (*Dr. Jack looks toward Belinda, who is busy grinding the grain from the new sack.*) A desprite, strange, crayture altogither. More like an animile thin human.

DR. JACK. (*Considering the matter.*) Why don't you talk to her?

McDONALD. Talk to her! I'd be wastin' me breath, man dear.

DR. JACK. No—she'd learn to read your lips. (*McDonald suprised.*)

McDONALD. Would she now! Read me lips!

DR. JACK. What's her name?

McDONALD. Her name? Well, by the Godfrey, I've clean fergot! They all call her the dummy around here. I'll have to look in me bible. Let's see, me wife—she passed on whin the child was born—she wanted her named after her grandmither. (*Scratching his chin.*) What in hell was that old hag's name?—Belinda. That's it, Belinda McDonald.

DR. JACK. Belinda! Why, that's a fine old Scotch name. There've been Belindas in Scotland since the days of the Scottish chiefs.

McDONALD. Her mither said—'twas a name to be proud of.

DR. JACK. But, Mr. McDonald, isn't this awful heavy work for your daughter—lifting those sacks?

McDONALD. Heavy work! You can't make a livin' on those farms here without a lot o' hands to help. Except fer me sister Maggie, here on a visit, I'm all alone and the girl must do a man's work. Well, I'm wastin' me time—and yours. (*He moves up to doorway.*)

DR. JACK. Would you mind if I talked to her for a moment?

McDONALD. Talk to her? Stay an' welcome. Good luck with the troot. I'd whip a fly with ye but I've got a fence to fix to kape me sheep home where they belong. (*McDonald exits.*)

DR. JACK. (*Looking at Belinda and saying to himself.*) You strange, tragic creature! I wonder of I could teach you. (*Calling.*) Belinda! (*No response from Belinda. He touches her shoulder and she cringes.*) Don't be afraid. —Come here; come, come. (*He beckons her toward the door. She pulls the lever which stops the grinder and moves timidly toward Dr. Jack.*) Where—are—the—fish? * (*He accompanies this with the sign for "fish." —Through-*

out the script an asterisk indicates the use of signs in conversation.) — The fish. * *(She still does not understand. He indicates his creel, and pretends to cast a fly and repeats the sign for fish. She understands and goes up to doorway and points off toward the pond.)* This * is the sign * the deaf * use * for "FISH" *. *(All these words are signed. Belinda tries it and is fairly successful.)* That's fine. *(A chicken is heard cackling and he points off.)* Look —chicken. *(Dr. Jack signs "Chicken" and she copies him.)* That's very good! *(Dr. Jack hears a bird singing somewhere in the trees and points out through the doorway at the flight of the bird.)* Look, a bird. *(Dr. Jack makes the sign for "BIRD" and Belinda copies it.)* Splendid! *(A cow is heard bawling in the pasture. Dr. Jack points off.)* Cow —— *(Belinda sees the cow and makes the sign for milking.)* That's it! —— *(Delightedly he comes back to his position opposite her.)* But there's more * to the sign * than that * — Look * Milking * and the Horns * *(Belinda copies him.)* Great! — Now let's see how much you can remember. (* *Dr. Jack points to his creel—the chickens—the bird—and the cow.)* Fish—Chicken—bird—cow. *(Belinda signs each one in turn.)* Perfect! Who says you can't learn? Belinda, I'm going to teach you to read *—— *(He signs. She doesn't grasp. He picks book off nail on beam and indicates lettering on the cover, repeating the * sign for read.)* To write * —— (* *Signed on an inner page of the book.)* And to talk * —— * —— *(Signed with a spiral from his mouth.)* To talk * —— (* *Sign repeated. Belinda makes a tentative spiral from her mouth, looks at him eagerly and points to herself questioningly. He nods. She is pleased and claps her hands.)* You're pleased? This is the sign when anything pleases * you. (* *Circular motion over the heart.)* Now, are you pleased *? (* *Signed again. She understands and imitates the sign.)* Belinda, I * am pleased * to meet * you *. *(All these signed.)* This is you * *(Indicating her with right forefinger.)* This is I *. (*Indicating himself with left forefinger.)* And I am pleased *. *(Circular motion over heart. Belinda laboriously makes signs and the Doctor translates.)* You—are—pleased * to meet—me. You're a wonderful pupil! *(He goes for his rod. Belinda touches him, indicates his creel, and makes the sign for "Fish" *.)* Yes, I'm going fishing; Belinda I * shall * see * you * soon *. *(Belinda does not understand.)* I * shall * see * you * again * soon *. *(He breaks off, goes up to entrance, turns to her.)* Goodbye * (* *Signed. He exits L. Belinda watches him go, she turns* *back, looks at her hands, experiments with the sign for "Fish," which she does well. Then very gracefully, she makes the sign for bird, and as it is completed, the song of the bobwhite in the trees is merrily heard as the Curtain Falls.)*

CURTAIN

ACT ONE

Scene 3

The Grist Mill.
The mill is full of young people. They are practicing steps for the Jig Contest. Hector McGuffey is fiddling old Scotch tunes. Andy McPhearson is doing a step with Lizzie Gordon. Locky McCormick is ringing Belinda's bell violently outside the mill door. Fergus grabs Stella and they do a sprightly hopping step. McCormick rings once more. Then Floyd seizes Stella and they do some fancy cuts, as McDonald enters angrily.)

McDONALD. What be ye trying to do McCormick, *(McDonald's first words stop all dancing. Dancers remain still.)* Shake the clapper out of that bell?
LOCKY. Where's me flour, Mac?
McDONALD. Ain't it done?
LOCKY. Not near, an' the old woman'll raise hell. I told you I'd pick it up on my way to the dance.
FLOYD. An' what aboot me buckwheat?
FERGUS. It ain't touched yet.
McDONALD. Ain't the dummy here to serve ye? *(Moving down to hopper.)*
FLOYD. No an' the Mill's shut down.
FERGUS. We've been waitin' around an hour.
ANDY. An' me oats, McDonald? How d'ye think we git butter fat in the village? I can't be fadin' the kittle roots all summer. *(McDonald gets the book from the nail.)*
McDONALD. Are ye all entered in the book right and proper? *(Thumbing through the book.)*
LOCKY. Sure, the dummy done that much. *(McDonald hangs book back on nail.)*

McDONALD. Well, McCormick comes first. The rest of ye needn't wait.

FLOYD. If that buckwheat ain't ground come noon tomorrow, Pa says to take it to Southport.

McDONALD. Take it an' wilcome. (*Going to door.*) I've enough on me mind without you and your wormy buckwheat. Where's the dummy?

ANDY. Down at the bridge with a bunch of bleeding hearts at her waist.

McGUFFEY. Watchin' the road like she expects a mimber of Parliment to come courtin' her.

FLOYD. An' every whip-stitch she combs her hair.

McDONALD. Combs her hair? (*He comes down nearer to them.*)

FERGUS. She's got a comb in her pocket.

FLOYD. Or a half a one anyway.

McDONALD. The girl's gone daft.

LOCKY. What d'ye expect? Her pa's half foolish. (*All burst into raucous laughter.*)

McDONALD. What's that! (*Everyone stops short.*) None of yer coddin' now, McCormick, or I'll break yer back.

LOCKY. (*He takes off his coat.*) Try it on Mac, I been pullin' two hundred traps a day, an' feelin' fit. (*Gracie and Lizzie sneak to one side out of danger. Andy and Fergus both back out of reach. McGuffey with his violin backs off. Stella holds her ground near Locky.*)

McDONALD. Proud of yer muscle be ye? Come on now, with yer big talk. (*McDonald starts for Locky and Stella runs between the two men.*)

STELLA. No! No! No! Mr. McDonald! (*She pushes Locky away.*) Stop it, d'ye hear? (*The others watch expectantly.*)

LOCKY. No, Mac. I'd spile me Sunday clothes. (*He picks up coat; Stella pulls coat away from him and brushes it off, turning the sleeves right side out. Hands it back and he gets into it.*)

McDONALD. All right, come around whin yer wearin' yer overalls. (*He crosses to go back to door.*) An' anyway I'd hate to humble ye afore Stella. Nae doot she thinks yer Samson hisself. She'll cut yer hair, from the build of her. An' hereafter kape a civil tongue in yer head. (*He starts to exit.*)

LOCKY. Thin git me flour done, or I'll cart it to Southport. (*Be-

linda enters. She wears shoes and stockings and a pretty calico dress.)

McDONALD. What the hell ye be doin' down there, thim bleedin' hearts at yer waist—combin' yer hair ——? *(He pulls her in and shoves her toward the hopper and the unfinished sacks of grain.)* Git back to yer work, yer lazy brat. *(She goes to the hopper. He follows her threatening to cuff her.)* What do ye think ye be—a lady of leisure. Git on with yer work. *(She turns on the water power and crouches by the open sack and starts to shovel grain into the hopper.)* There now, McCormick. She'll have yer flour done in a jeffy. *(He moves back toward the door.)*

LOCKY. All right, Mac.—I'll let you off this time.

McDONALD. Let me off indade! Wheniver yer ready I'll larn ye a trick or two. Well, have a good time at the dance, young folks. Forty years ago I might have larned ye a jig or two meself! *(He does a step or two. All laugh and applaud except Belinda, who is intent on her work.)*

McGUFFEY, FLOYD, FERGUS, ANDY. Come on, Mac—show us some more steps.

McDONALD. I gotta milk me cows. *(He grins, waves and exits.)*

FLOYD. Pick it up, McGuffey! *(Mcguffey tightens his fiddle strings a bit, while the boys try to imitate the steps McDonald showed them.)*

STELLA. Locky, don't you iver go annoying him again—or I'll hold no more traffic with ye.

LOCKY. Take it aisey, Stella—I kin take care of meself. *(Floyd, Lizzie, McPherson and Mabel are jigging with the boys while McGuffey fiddles.)*

FERGUS. Come on, Stella, and jig with me. *(Fergus and Stella do a jig together. Belinda, having emptied one sack, crosses to account book on the nail, makes a mark in it. Then returns to the hopper and starts on another sack. She becomes conscious of the jigging. She watches the feet of the dancers and tries to imitate a step or two but can't make it. She thinks of McGuffey and his fiddle—crosses to him and places her hand on the fiddle, getting the rhythm and thus is able to move her feet in time with the music. Locky has watched her through all this.)*

LOCKY. *(Stopping the dancing and calling everybody's attention to Belinda.)* Look at that, will ye! The Dummy hears through her fingers. *(Belinda becomes aware of them all watching, stops trying*

27

to keep time, and goes back to her work.) By the Godfrey, she'll niver git all them sacks done tonight. That's a sack of mine she's workin' on now.

FLOYD. No use hangin' 'round here.

STELLA. Lizzie, if we stay in here, we'll all be kivered with flour dust. (*She takes her hat off, looks at it, and blows the dust off.*)

FERGUS. Come on, Andy, Floyd. We'll get the rig. (*Boys exit, Locky watches Belinda, who goes on with her work as if no one were there.*)

STELLA. (*To Lizzie.*) Besides I promised I'd help Gladys with her dress. Hurry, Locky.

LOCKY. I got to git this flour. The old woman will be highsterical.

LIZZIE. Let Locky wait for his flour. I've seen his mither when she gits riled.

STELLA. (*Pulling on her hat.*) I want him to come with me. (*McGuffey grabs Lizzie by the hand and pulls her after him—they exit.*)

LOCKY. You go along, Stella, 'Gin yer half way there, the flour'll be done an' with that mare of mine I'll be there afore yer tay's drunk. (*Taking Stella up toward the door.*)

STELLA. (*In a low voice.*) You kape away from that Dummy!

LOCKY. The Dummy? Me?

STELLA. I saw ye takin' in her legs, and sizin' her up like you was undressin' her!

LOCKY. Aw, Stella!

STELLA. One thing—she couldn't tell on ye, but kape away from her if you want to marry me.

LOCKY. Aw! Go on! Jealous of a dummy! Woman, I'm plumb ashamed of ye! (*He turns her and slaps her rear as she exits.*) Tell Gladys to save me some of them raisin cookies. (*McGuffey enters for his violin.*)

McGUFFEY. I forgot me fiddle. (*He puts the fiddle and bow in the case and runs out with it.*)

LOCKY. (*Watching Belinda, gets an idea and calls after McGuffey.*) Hey, McGuffey!

McGUFFEY. (*Offstage.*) What?

LOCKY. Come here a minute.

McGUFFEY. (*Returning.*) What do ye want?

LOCKY. Lend us yer fiddle for a spell, will ye?

McGUFFEY. What do you want with it?

LOCKY. I want to larn it.
McGUFFEY. Well, be chary of it. I don't want it busted. I'm gittin' a dollar and a half fer fiddlin' tonight.
LOCKY. I'll be careful. I'll bring it over to the dance with me.
McGUFFEY. Well—don't be late.
LOCKY. I won't. (*McGuffey surrenders the case and exits. Locky takes violin and bow from case, sits down on pile of sacks and pretends to play, using the back of the bow on the strings, going through the motions of playing but making no sound. Belinda, busy at the work, does not see him. He stamps heavily on the floor with one foot. Belinda feels the vibration and looks toward him. Sees him playing the violin apparently as McGuffey did, smiles, and goes toward Locky. Locky, making his feet go as if dancing.*) You wanna dance? (*She reaches out a timid hand and touches the violin as he pretends to play, but feels no vibration, is puzzled, disappointed, and draws back. Locky stops pretending to play. He grabs for her hand. She retreats.*) Come here! I want to talk to ye. (*With gesture to his open mouth, Belinda makes the sign for "talk".*) What's that? (*He copies her gesture. She thinks he is signing to her to talk. Belinda repeats the sign for "talk" with the meaning "I can talk." She makes the sign for "fish."*) What's all them monkeydoodles? (*She makes the sign for "chicken."*) Yer awful comical, Dummy. (*She makes the sign for "bird" with her arms outstretched.*) But, by the Godfrey, yer cute. (*He grabs her around the waist and draws her to him kissing her violently on the mouth.*) Did ye like that? (*She pushes herself free and backs away from him.*) Oh, ye're scared! . . . Well, I'm thinkin' that was yer first kiss! I caught a seagull oncet, and it had the same scared look. Don't be frightened, girl. (*He edges towards her.*) I kin hear yer heart thumpin' way over here. Ye didn't twig what magic lies in a pair o' lips, did ye? Come here while I give ye a rale one. (*He grabs for her. She springs away—points to the violin on the floor and motions to him to play it for her to dance, moving her feet.*) Oh —— Ye want to dance, do ye? (*He picks up the violin and pretends to play it, with the back of the bow and making no sounds. He smiles at her and shuffles his feet in dance steps. She is encouraged. She comes to him, slowly, reaches out her hand and touches the violin but she again feels no vibration and is puzzled. This is Locky's chance and he seizes her around the waist, drops bow and violin and catches her in his arms. He attempts to kiss*

her. *She tries her best to avoid it, struggling to be free of him, but he forces her back on the pile of sacks and rips open her dress. She reaches desperately for the bell on the old chair near the door, but Locky holds her powerless. The lights Fade Quickly and the Curtain Comes Down.)*

CURTAIN

END OF ACT ONE

ACT TWO

Scene 1

Black McDonald's Kitchen.
A back door gives, beyond the back porch, a slightly different view of the mill pond. Over the door is a shot gun held in two small crotches from some tree. On the right, against the back wall and window, a sink with a pump for water. Under the sink a cupboard. Down right, a wood stove. Down left, a door to another room. Up left, a door to the upstairs. Between the doors a pantry. Table, chairs, a horsehair sofa, a frame for making a hooked mat.
At the Rise: Maggie is sitting at R. end of the sofa at a spinning wheel. McDonald is in his chair, R. end of table C., reading family Bible.

MAGGIE. Spinnin's a chore the Dummy could do. Bakin' and churnin' and washin' wool: me back's near broke! (*Her hair falls loose. She rises, goes up to sink. She opens cupboard under L. of sink, takes a nail from a pail and pins up her hair with it.*) I'd be better off home to Southport. . . . Did ye hear me?
McDONALD. Shut yer trap, woman. Ye've got more gabble nor a goose.
MAGGIE. (*Staring back from her spinning.*) What are ye all spruced up fer? A clean shirt on in the middle of the week. I don't understand ye at all, John McDonald, since ye've been hobnobbin' with that doctor. (*McDonald reads a moment in silence. Then rises, puts Bible on table; turns and goes to stove; knocks out his pipe. He stands thoughtful, his back to the stove.*)
McDONALD. I driv round by the Church today. First time in fifteen years. Had a look at me wife's grave. All kivered with weeds. The haidstone broke down: "ANN—BELOVED WIFE OF JOHN McDONALD." Just a wee thing she were. Do ye remember her, Maggie?

MAGGIE. Much too good fer ye. An' far too young.

McDONALD. A wistful lass. Awful mild she was. Kind of whispered whin she talked. (*He turns and puts his pipe on shelf to* L. *of stove.*) Where's Belinda?

MAGGIE. (*Stopping her spinning.*) What!

McDONALD. Where's Belinda?

MAGGIE. Are ye in yer right mind, John McDonald?

McDONALD. Ay!

MAGGIE. Ye mean the Dummy?

McDONALD. I mean Belinda. That's her name. 'Tis writ in the book. (*He picks up the Bible from the table and carries it to the little table up* L. *between door and pantry.*)

MAGGIE. Niver till this night have I heard ye call her by that name. Nor no one else.

McDONALD. Where d'ye suppose she be?

MAGGIE. Well, since the doctor ain't here to kape her from her work, she's gone to her bed I'm thinkin'. (*She resumes her spinning.*)

McDONALD. (*He drops* D. *to chair* L. *of table and sits.*) I promised her mither I'd look after her, and I ain't done it.

MAGGIE. She's always had enough to eat.

McDONALD. She's comin' on to womanhood.

MAGGIE. She's been a woman these five years, if ye had any since—which ye haven't.

McDONALD. I suppose she'll be wantin' a mate.

MAGGIE. Where would *she* git one?

McDONALD. Yer right. Where to find one—that's the question. Deef and dumb as she be—poor girl.

MAGGIE. None of the byes runnin' in and out of the mill would marry her.

McDONALD. Nay—and they're a dirty bunch, that rotten click from East Pond, the McGuiggans and rest. I don't trust 'em none—if yer twig what I mean. I ought to warn her.

MAGGIE. Aye—ye should.

McDONALD. She should of wint to school.

MAGGIE. Aw!

McDONALD. There's schools fer the deef and dumb.

MAGGIE. That's more of that Doctor's talk.

McDONALD. That's why I'm reproachin' meself. The whole thing come over me all of a sudden standin' there in the Churchyard

today. Strange how a man kin forgit. (*Belinda enters from upstairs. She crosses to little stool over* L., *takes it down stage by the stove and works at her needle-point frame.*)
MAGGIE. There she is now. She slips aboot so quiet she gives me the creeps.
McDONALD. Git in to yer room, will ye, woman? I have an awful yearnin' to talk to her.
MAGGIE. Talk to her?
McDONALD. That can be done.
MAGGIE. I won't stay where I'm not wanted. The way I'm shoved around you'd think I was some poor relation. (*She exits* D. L. *carrying out her spinning wheel. McDonald rises, goes around table to* R. *of Belinda. She starts in fright and springs up, retreating towards* L.)
McDONALD. (*He advances a step.*) Don't be frightened! (*She retreats again to the sofa. He puts out his hand for the needlework. She crouches with it on the* R. *end of the sofa. He goes and takes it from her. She looks hurt. He takes needlework to the light of the lamp on table* C., *and examines it.*) Well, now—that's handsome—Bluebells—Bluebells of Scotland. Very pretty they be too. They writ a song aboot thim. (*He hands the frame back to Belinda, who clutches it to her.*) Ah, Belinda—child—how pretty ye be. I been too busy to notice—or too selfish, I'm thinkin'. 'Tis a bitter grief ye nay kin talk. What a cozy time we'd make of it—just we two togither. I know ye hear naught o' what I say nor understand one jot of it. But it aises me speŕrit to talk to ye. (*He holds his hand out to her. She takes it timidly. He squeezes it in a friendly way. She withdraws it, not knowing what he means.*) Of course ye don't understand. (*He rises, moves below table a step.*) But this ye kin understand: Now look: Ye know the mill—the mill. (*He makes the gesture of pulling the lever, and the rotating motion of the discs.*) Well, hereafter, I do the grinding. (*He points to himself and repeats the motions. Belinda cocks her head in query.*) Aye, I'll do it. The work is too hard fer ye. Thim heavy sacks —— (*He goes through the motion of lifting a heavy sack, and dumping the contents into a hopper: and suddenly pretends to wince, catching the small of his back.*) I'm afraid ye'll hurt yeself, child. But me—I'm as strong as a bull. (*Puffs out his chest, and thumps it with a resounding thwack, and indicates that she shall feel his biceps.*) Feel. . . . (*She puts her hand on it.*) But you. . . . (*He

feels her arm.) My hiven, you're soft as a baby. (*He moves a step down stage.*) I'll attind to all that in the future. That part is aisey —— But, Belinda, child, what's to become of ye? I'd like to warn ye—aboot that dirty click from East Pond, but how am I to do it, God Almighty only knows!—But enough fer tonight. (*Brightening.*) Now what kin I do to amuse ye? . . . (*A happy thought strikes him.*) I know . . . (*He calls off.*) Maggie! Maggie . . .
MAGGIE. (*Offstage.*) What is it, man?
McDONALD. Be there any corn left from Christmas?
MAGGIE. Look for yerself. 'Tis in the pantry.
McDONALD. (*Going to the pantry.*) And kin ye find the popper?
MAGGIE. (*Entering.*) Ye broke the handle off it the last time ye used it. Use the frying pan.
McDONALD. Come on, daughter, we're goin' to have a shindig. (*He finds the bag of corn in the pantry and gives it to Belinda. He then finds the frying pan and puts it on the stove.*) Maggie, where's the salt and butter?
MAGGIE. Salt's on the shelf in front of your eyes. Where do you think it is? (*She gets the butter from pantry which she places on table.*) Wastin' good butter poppin' corn to amuse the dummy. (*Belinda puts a bit of butter in the frying pan, removes a lid from the stove—places the frying pan over the fire, then dumps in the corn, gives the empty bag to McDonald, covers the frying pan with a tin cover. McDonald blows up the bag and as Maggie stoops to straighten the blanket on the sofa, he pops it behind her back and she is so startled she nearly jumps out of her skin.*) Oh ——! Up to yer silly tricks! Wastin' a good paper bag! (*The corn has begun to pop, can be heard hitting the tin cover over the frying pan. Belinda gets a bowl.*)
McDONALD. (*To Maggie.*) Git to bed, woman! Yer a damper on the party. I'm happier tonight then I bin in many a day. (*Maggie exits to room* D. L. *Belinda dumps the popcorn from the frying pan into the bowl, puts the frying pan on the back of stove, replaces the lid to the stove, sprinkles some salt over the pop corn in the bowl and offers it to McDonald. McDonald takes a handful and stuffs it in his mouth, snaps his fingers as he chews.*) Umm! Good. (*Belinda, pleased because he is pleased, takes a kernel of the popcorn herself. McDonald continues to snap his fingers, and says* ——) Come on, daughter, we're goin' to dance. (*He does some jig steps, with a stamp in them. Belinda feels the stamp, sees the move-*

ment of his feet and tries to do likewise. After a little practice She follows the beat of his feet very well.) Swing yer partner! (He takes her by the arm and wheels her around as—Dr. Jack enters U. He hangs up his coat on a peg to L. of Door.)

DR. JACK. Well!—— Having a party?

McDONALD. Come in, Doctor—and jine the fun. I took yer advice—goin' to let her ease up on the work—thought I'd give her a little shindy. (Belinda signs: "I am pleased to meet you." McDonald sees it.) What's all that business?

DR. JACK. That means: "I * am pleased * to meet * you *. (* Signed.)

McDONALD. Well, now!

DR. JACK. A very intelligent girl, Mr. McDonald—this daughter of yours. You'll be surprised how quickly she learns.

McDONALD. (Turning to sink.) Yes, but what kin ye taitch her?

DR. JACK. Practically everything. (Belinda comes to Dr. Jack with popcorn bowl and offers it to him. He takes some.) Thank you *. (* Signed. Belinda offers popcorn to McDonald, who takes some. He has watched the sign.)

McDONALD. Thank you *, Belinda. —Did I do that right? (* Signed.)

DR. JACK. Perfectly.

McDONALD. That's strange. I don't remimber iver thankin' her for anythin' before in her life, but I'll remimber to do so in the future. (He repeats the sign for "thank you" to himself.) Tell me some more about this business.

DR. JACK. (Taking book from pocket, and bringing it to R. of table above McDonald, who moves up to chair R. of table.) Here's the text book we've been working from. It's a sign language invented a couple of hundred years ago for the deaf by a Frenchman, —Abbe de L'Epée. (Belinda drops back to stove, sits on her little stool with popcorn bowl.)

McDONALD. For instance ——?

DR. JACK. (Dropping round to L. of table.) For instance, this would be "man" *. (* Signed in two parts: tipping the hat and the height of a man. Belinda repeats it.)

McDONALD. I twig—tipping the hat. (Getting it first from Dr. Jack, then from Belinda.)

DR. JACK. (He indicates height of a man.) And the height of a man . . . This would be "gentleman" *. (* Signed in two parts:

complete sign for "man" and indication of the "ruffle.") This indicates the ruffle, which the gentleman used to wear. "Gentleman" * . . . (* *Signed. Belinda copies.*)

McDONALD. Well, now what would Woman be?

DR. JACK. (*He runs the thumb of his right hand down the back of his right cheek—and holds his hand at the height of a woman.*) This. The bonnet string—and the height of a woman. (* *Signed.*) "Woman" *. (*Belinda copies.*)

McDONALD. Well! By the Godfrey, that's clever!! And what would father be?

DR. JACK. This sign for "man"—followed by this:—as if holding a baby. . . . (*He touches his thumb and forefinger to his forehead, then extends both arms forward and open as if holding a baby.*) "Father" *. (* *Signed. Belinda copies.*)

McDONALD. That would be me!

DR. JACK. Yes. (*McDonald makes a sign for "Father" turning as he does so, and seeing Belinda seated on stool by the stove downstage, making the sign for "Mother"—the bonnet string and gesture of holding a baby.*)

McDONALD. And that would be "mither"?

DR. JACK. That's right.

McDONALD. (*Running toward door* D. L.) Maggie! Maggie!

MAGGIE. (*Off Left.*) What is it?

McDONALD. Come here! I've got something!

DR. JACK. Mac—this would be "grandfather" *. Father once removed. "Ancestors" *. On into the past. (* *Signed.*)

McDONALD. Well, that's remarkable! (*Enter Maggie in nightgown.*)

MAGGIE. What's the matter? What's got into you?

McDONALD. (*Seizing blanket from sofa and covers her up.*) Kivver yerself up, woman—yer half naked.

MAGGIE. Shame on ye, calling me out here with the doctor in the room.

McDONALD. (*Making sign for "Woman."*) Maggie,—what would this mean? —Look sharp now—think hard!

MAGGIE. Ye've got the toothache.

McDONALD. Toothache? 'Tis the sign language. It means lady: the bonnet string. D'ye twig?

MAGGIE. I twig yer actin' awful childish.

McDONALD. (*Making sign for "Gentleman."*) What would this be?
MAGGIE. Don't be wavin' yer hands at me. I'm no dummy.
McDONALD. Git back to bed, woman —— Ye've a faculty for sayin' the wrong thing. (*He snatches the blanket from her and throws it on couch.*)
MAGGIE. Have ye gone plumb daft, John McDonald? (*She exits* D. L.)
McDONALD. I think this deserves a cilibration. Would you like a dish?
DR. JACK. A dish?
McDONALD. Whin I say "Dish" I mane somethin' stronger than tay.
DR. JACK. Why yes. —I'll have a dish. (*McDonald fetches a demijohn and two glasses from the pantry.*)
McDONALD. (*As he fills the glasses.*) This has won a heap of battles for the British Navy. (*He gives a glass to Dr. Jack.*) Here, man—that'll put hair on yer chest. (*They raise their glasses, touch them and drink to each other's health. The Doctor chokes and runs to the sink for water.*) What's the matter, man?
DR. JACK. What's in it?
McDONALD. Oh, some pertatie pealins, molasses, mash and a few other odds and ends. I got a still back in the woods.
DR. JACK. (*Looking at contents of glass.*) Good God! (*Pumps some water in his glass at sink, then drains it, and hands glass back to McDonald.*)
McDONALD. (*Placing glasses on sink.*) Well, I'll be sayin' goodnight. I got a hard day tomorrow. (*Going to staircase door* U. L. *and opening it.*)
DR. JACK. Good night, Mr. McDonald.
McDONALD. (*Indicating Belinda.*) Doctor, I've been neglectin' my jooty to this girl. (*Crossing back to Dr. Jack* U. C.) Not till tonight did I realize how much, or the tragedy of it. It must be a terrible thing—this livin' in silence. I've so much to say to her—so much a father should say—but I've no the means.
DR. JACK. I'll give you the means. I'm going to teach her to read, to write, and to talk.
McDONALD. TALK! Be ye serious, man?
DR. JACK. Of course, I'm serious.
McDONALD. If you can do that, you're a worker of miracles.

37

DR. JACK. I'll have her talking before the year's out.
McDONALD. Good night, Belinda!
DR. JACK. Would you like to say that so she'd understand you?
McDONALD. I certainly would.
DR. JACK. Well, it's this: "Good night" *. (* *Good and "night" signed separately.*) You see, this represents the horizon. (*Indicating his left arm, raising it horizontally.*) This is morning *, the sun coming up over the horizon. This is noon *, the sun directly overhead, —afternoon * —— (**With his right arm he indicates the sun midway between Zenith and horizon.*) Evening * —the sun nearer the horizon. And night *—the sun below the horizon. Good-day *—Good night *. (* *Signs these two.*)
McDONALD. Good night * —— (**Signed.*) --Daughter? (*He makes the "bonnet-string" sign for "woman" looking at Dr. Jack questioningly.*)
DR. JACK. No, that's "Woman!" This is "daughter!" * (* *Signed.*)
McDONALD. Good night * —Daughter *. (*Belinda signs, rather mystified and quite timidly, "Good night"—"Father." Translating.*) "Good night—Father." —That's the first time she's ever called me that. (*With a pleased chuckle he picks up his rum and exits upstairs.*) Well—now! (*He leaves the door open.*)
DR. JACK. Now, Belinda—your lessons! * (**Signed. He seats himself at the table and prepares. Belinda is touched by her father's kindness and goes slowly to the door, closing it, and lingering there.*) Come, Belinda! We must get to work! * (* *Signed. Belinda comes slowly D. to chair L. of table and sits. Impulsively she seizes the Doctor's hand and kisses it. Dr. Jack is slightly embarrassed at this demonstration. He raises her head and looks into her eyes.*) Why, you funny child! (*Then rallies her.*) Belinda—come—come now! (*He holds up the Alphabet cards. Shows her the letters.*) Your work—the alphabet. (*Then hides the card.*) "A." (*She makes the symbol for "A."*) Right.—"B." (*She hesitates. Tries to peek. He hides the card. She signs it correctly.*) Correct.—"C." (*She makes "C" beautifully.*) Right.—"D." (*The Lights Fade Out as she is making "D."*)

ACT TWO

Scene 2

The Kitchen.
Dr. Jack enters from up stairs and closes the door as Maggie comes in from the outdoors in a floppy straw hat, carrying a bunch of carrots.

DR. JACK. Oh, Miss McDonald ——
MAGGIE. (*She is weary and surly.*) Good day, Doctor.
DR. JACK. I finished my rounds and stopped by to fish the mill stream a while ago.
MAGGIE. I saw ye there.
DR. JACK. Belinda came along. She'd been blueberrying.
MAGGIE. She don't do much else these days.
DR. JACK. She wasn't feeling very well, so I brought her home—made her go upstairs and lie down.
MAGGIE. In the middle of the day? What ails her?
DR. JACK. She has a headache amongst other things. Tell me, has she been eating regularly?
MAGGIE. As regular as the rest of us. She don't fancy her food none. Just picks at it. Guess it ain't good enough for her no more.
DR. JACK. What do you mean by that?
MAGGIE. I mean all the grand ideas you been puttin' into her haid. If you want to do us a favor—me brother and me—you'll give up tryin' to educate that girl. 'Tain't fair to the people she's supposed to be helpin'. I'm doin' the work of six.
DR. JACK. I'm sorry to hear that, of course, but I think Belinda is doing her share and more. That girl is sick, Miss McDonald—that's why she hasn't any appetite.
MAGGIE. She don't do enough to git up an appetite—not since you made her father take over the mill.
DR. JACK. I merely told him that lifting those sacks was too strenuous for her. You still have her carrying those buckets of skim milk, butter milk or what not to feed the pigs. They must weigh thirty pounds a piece.
MAGGIE. (*Flaring up.*) What do you think she is—a hothouse flower? There were no complaints till you came around. She did

39

her work like the rest of us—like we all have to, if we want to kape a roof over our haids.

DR. JACK. You're not very fond of Belinda, are you?

MAGGIE. I was civil to her till you started makin' a lady of her.

DR. JACK. Well, you're the only woman she knows, and she may be in need of your sympathy and help.

MAGGIE. My help?

DR. JACK. Miss McDonald, I'm pretty certain Belinda is pregnant.

MAGGIE. What?!

DR. JACK. I've suspected it for some time, but there are symptoms now which make me practically certain.

MAGGIE. The poor girl. Oh, you don't know what this may mean. Me brother—for all he's a rough one—is a man of principle and a proud one. If he discovers this, I think he'd like to kill her!

DR. JACK. Of course, there's the chance I may be mistaken. I have my bag in the rig, I'll run down and get her something for that headache. (*McDonald enters u. He is very weary and glum. Dr. Jack brightens his tone for McDonald.*) Oh, hello, Mac.

McDONALD. Good day, Doctor. Did ye come up for some troot?

DR. JACK. Yes, I hope to get you a nice mess for dinner. Oh—here's your quarter. (*Taking coin from pocket.*)

McDONALD. Oh, fergit it, man.

DR. JACK. Oh, no—take it. You must take my quarter. I won't have any luck with that quarter in my pocket. (*He places the quarter on the table.*) Now, just watch me—I'll fill the creel! (*Laughs jokingly and exits u.*)

McDONALD. The Doctor's only coddin', but I don't mind sayin' I can use ivery quarter I can lay me hands on. Ye'd best be gittin back to Southport, woman. I won't be able to fade ye soon, the way things is goin'. (*He puts the quarter in his pocket.*)

MAGGIE. Oh, stuff and nonsense! 'Tain't like you, John McDonald, to give in when you have a little bad luck.

McDONALD. Take a look at that grainfield. 'Tain't worth the harvestin'. The mustard got the start of me this Spring, and choked out the wheat.

MAGGIE. Well, you were short-handed.

McDONALD. I lost a foal—two cows dead with milk fever—and the hay's so thick with white dasies the kittle won't eat it unless they're starvin'!

MAGGIE. Thought ye was goin' to town to fetch yer new harness.

McDONALD. I bin in. Pocket wouldn't let me take it without the cash. What's more, he's stopped all me credit.

MAGGIE. Stopped yer credit!

McDONALD. I bin runnin' a bill at the store for siveral years now. He charges me interest and it's been mountin' and mountin'. And I ain't been able to catch up with it.

MAGGIE. But, man dear, if he's stopped yer credit, what will ye do for groceries—fer tay and sugar and salt and the like?

McDONALD. God knows, woman! I'm near daft with worry!

MAGGIE. Well, now—that's no way to be! Somethin'll turn up—somethin' always does. They say there's a fine run o' herrin'. Git the nets out. We might salt down a couple of barrels. (*Belinda enters from upstairs. She is rocky. She goes to the pails. Maggie sees her and tries to stop her.*) Here—wait a minute, child—I'll take those. —Oh! (*But she is gone, not hearing Maggie.*) That's too bad.

McDONALD. What's the trouble?

MAGGIE. Nothin'. I was just going to carry the buckets for the Dummy.

McDONALD. The whey for the pigs? She's late with it. (*He goes up to the door, U. C.*)

MAGGIE. She's got a sick headache. The Doctor told her to lay down.

McDONALD. God! I could do with the help of a man on this farm. I work from four o'clock in the mornin' till dusk, year in and year out. And what's a body got to show fer it? The first John McDonald owned the whole King's County. And what have I got—eighty-six acres, and half of that over-run with sheep pizen. Well, I'd best be at the grain. Will ye help me with the bindin'?

MAGGIE. I'll ketch up with ye. (*Belinda returns with the empty buckets. She goes to sink to wash them. As she lifts them she drops them and doubles up in pain.*) Here, pet, let Maggie help ye. (*Belinda moves to chair back of table—gets a stab in the back.*)

McDONALD. What's wrong with her? (*He leads her to the couch.*)

MAGGIE. I told ye she was out of sorts. (*She pumps glass of water and brings it to McDonald.*) Here, here's some water for her. (*McDonald lifts the glass to Belinda's lips. She takes a sip and then refuses more, burying her face in the head of the couch. He watches her.*) The doctor says she's been working too hard.

McDONALD. I done me best to be aisy with the work. The chores ain't much.

MAGGIE. Now, John, you go out in the grain field and lave her with me. The doctor's bringing her some medicine. (*Belinda doubles up in pain.*)

McDONALD. Wait a minute—that ain't just a headache. She's in agony! She's come down with somethin'.

MAGGIE. Will ye please lave her to me and the doctor? (*McDonald rises and goes to Maggie.*)

McDONALD. What are ye tryin' to make a mystery of it fer? She's me daughter—I've a right to know if it's anythin' serious!

MAGGIE. Well, get a hold of yerself, John. The doctor says she's goin' to have a child.

McDONALD. What's that ye say?

MAGGIE. It's no use tryin' to kape it from ye, since this thing's happened. (*Pause.*)

McDONALD. (*Goes back to foot of couch.*) Good God Almighty —what swine done this?

MAGGIE. Hold yer timper, John!

McDONALD. Hold me timper! What kind of a father do you think I am? Who's been at her? She's never off the place. She ain't been in the mill since I took over the work. And none of that rabble from East Pond dare show their face here!

MAGGIE. This must have happened some time ago—when she was there alone.

McDONALD. (*Sitting on couch and drawing her up.*) Belinda— child ——

MAGGIE. Be gintle with her—John.

McDONALD. Listen, child—who is it that's harmed ye? —Who is it that's hurt ye?

MAGGIE. She don't understand ye!

McDONALD. Belinda—try to understand. They say ye're goin' to be a mither —— Can't ye understand? (*He takes the calendar off the wall. Shows her the picture of the Madonna.*) A MITHER! —Which one of that dirty click done this?

MAGGIE. She don't know what yer talkin' aboot.

McDONALD. (*Rising and facing Maggie again.*) Don't be a fool, woman. She's not a baby in arms for all she's deaf! And why don't she let me know if some man was annyin' her? She had the bell. She knew I'd be there in a moment. She understands all right. She's tryin' to shield someone. But she'll tell me his name whether she wants to or not.

MAGGIE. How do ye expict her to do that?

McDONALD. I'll find a way. Maggie! Give me that account book from the mill.

MAGGIE. (*Going* R., *looking helplessly.*) The account book ——

McDONALD. (*Impatiently going to drawer in table* C., *taking out book and coming to Belinda.*) That account book! (*He shows her a page.*) Now then! Who done it? Was it him?

MAGGIE. How can she tell from that?

McDONALD. She knows every page by heart! Kape out of this, woman! Is it one of them McGuiggan scum that's had ye? Is it? (*He shows her another page.*) Is it McGinnis? (*He shows her another page.*) Or O'Keefe? (*He shows her another page.*) McCormick! Is it him that's had ye? (*He shows her another page.*) There's the book. Pick him out! Pick out the man, or, by God! (*He throws book on the floor.*) I'll bate it out of ye! (*He rips off his belt. Maggie rushes in and grasps his wrist, turning him round, way from the couch.*)

MAGGIE. John! John! Don't do it!

McDONALD. Pick him out!

MAGGIE. Don't do it!

McDONALD. Kape away, woman, kape away! (*Dr. Jack enters* U.)

MAGGIE. Doctor! Doctor! Kape him off!

DR. JACK. (*Coming to* L. *of McDonald and grasping his arm.*) What the hell's the matter with you? Get a hold of yourself, Mac.

McDONALD. Take yer hands off me! Ye'll be needed there! (*Dr. Jack releases him gradually, and follows McDonald's glance and gestures toward Belinda. He goes quickly to her, as McDonald exits* U.)

DR. JACK. What happened, Maggie?

MAGGIE. She took the buckets before I could stop her. I had to tell me brother what you said, and he was tryin' to discover the man's name. (*She places belt on table.*)

DR. JACK. He didn't strike her?

MAGGIE. No.

DR. JACK. We must get her to bed.

MAGGIE. I'll go up and have things ready. (*She exits upstairs* L. *Belinda signs: "Why is my father angry?"*)
DR. JACK. (*Translating.*) Why is your father angry? (*As he starts to lift her in his arms the Lights Fade Out.*) Come, dear.

ACT TWO

Scene 3

Belinda's Bedroom.
A corner of the attic with a dormer window, a spool bed with patchwork quilt, small bureau with a kerosene lamp on it, a vase with some flowers in it.
Maggie is sitting, watching the sleeping Belinda. Belinda stirs. She turns restlessly to one side, then to the other, and then she starts up in bed as if in terror.

MAGGIE. (*Going quickly to her, she gently places her on the pillow.*) Don't stir yerself. Rest quiet. Take it aisey.— (*She goes to door* L. *and calls down.*) Doctor! Doctor!
DR. JACK. (*Downstairs.*) Yes, Maggie?
MAGGIE. She's awake now. (*She turns up to lamp and raises the wick. The room becomes more brightly illuminated.*)
DR. JACK. (*Enters and crosses to* L. *of bed.*) Did you give her the medicine?
MAGGIE. Not yet. 'Tis here in the glass. (*She hands the glass and a spoon to Dr. Jack, who gives Belinda a spoonful. Belinda makes a face. Maggie takes medicine and replaces it.*)
DR. JACK. (*He feels Belinda's pulse.*) Feeling better? (*Belinda signs: "Very tired."*) Of course you're tired. (*He feels her forehead.*)
MAGGIE. How is she, Doctor?
DR. JACK. I can't quite tell yet, Maggie; but I think she's going to be all right.
MAGGIE. Can she have something to eat now?
DR. JACK. Some of that broth, if you don't mind.
MAGGIE. I'll go and git it. (*She exits* L. *Belinda signs: "Who will do my work?"*)
DR. JACK. Your work? * Your * father * will * do * it. (* *Signed. Belinda signs: "My father is angry with me."*) No. He *

44

is not * angry *. He * was * worried *. He * has * lots * of worries *. He wants * to ask * your * forgiveness *. Do * you * forgive * him *? (* *Signed. Belinda looks resentfully in the direction of the door. Then she shrinks and a thought comes to her She signs: "You taught me."*) I taught you? I taught * you * what *? (* *Signed. Belinda signs laboriously, and the doctor interprets.*) "Forgive—us—our trespasses—as—we—forgive—those—who—trespass against us." You dear child!

MAGGIE. (*She re-enters with a cup of broth. She offers it to Belinda.*) Here, child, some nice broth Maggie's made fer ye. (*Belinda rejects it with an apologetic face.*)

DR. JACK. Try * it *—It * will * do * you * good *. (* *Signed. Belinda still refuses.*)

MAGGIE. (*Setting cup aside on bureau.*) She's not hungry.

DR. JACK. Later maybe. (*Sound of a Shivaree—music, laughter, and voices—is heard from outside.*) What's going on, Maggie?

MAGGIE. Highjinks over to the Aitken Farm. That Locky McCormick got married today.

DR. JACK. Oh, yes—to Stella Maguire. She used to work for me.

MAGGIE. The young folks of the sittlement are givin' 'em a shivaree.

DR. JACK. (*Looking out of the window.*) A shivaree? I've never been to one.

MAGGIE. It's just a lot of mischief to kape the newlyweds out of bed. Probably got a cow bell tied to the springs to get them out of it once they're in it!

DR. JACK. What are those spurts of flame?

MAGGIE. Oh that! Well, the byes take a mouthful of kerosene ile, and as they blow it out they touch a match to it—blow the flame through the windys—set the curtains afire—or the girl's hair. 'Tis all in good mean fun.

DR. JACK. McCormick's done well for himself. Stella's a fine girl.

MAGGIE. She comes of nice people. Well, I'll say goodnight, doctor. (*To Belinda.*) Good night, dear. (*Belinda makes a sign of query to Dr. Jack. He signs "Good night" to her. She signs "Good night" to Maggie.*) Don't let anything happen to her. I bin pretty brusque with her—awful crotchety.

DR. JACK. You've been kind and helpful enough tonight to make up for a great deal, Maggie.

MAGGIE. Well, us McDonalds—we're high tempered. We fight amongst ourselves—but let trouble come from outside—and we stick together. (*She exits* L. *Another burst from the shivaree. Dr. Jack looks out of the window. Belinda touches him and signs: "What is going on out there?"*)
DR. JACK. What's going on outside? That's a party *. (* *Signed. Belinda signs: "I've never been to a party."*) You've never been to a party? No, you haven't had much fun. (*She touches him in query.*) I said: You * haven't * had * much * fun *. You * have been * very * lonely *. But * you * won't * be * lonely * any * more *. (* *Signed. She looks to him in query.*) Belinda—You * are to * become * a mother *. (* *Signed. She looks at him in awe. She slowly makes the sign for "Mother."*) Yes *. You *. (* *Signed. She shows amazement and fear. She sits up and looks down at her body. Then a great understanding comes over her face. She looks up as if in rapturous anticipation. She signs: "I want a boy."*) Oh, you want a boy, do you? Why * not * a girl *? (* *Signed. She signs: "No—a boy!"*) All right—we * shall hope * for a boy. (* *Signed. The Shivaree noise swells as the lights* ——)

FADE OUT

ACT TWO

Scene 4

The Kitchen.
There is a cradle D. R. C., L. *of stove. McDonald is seated at* L. *of table with the mill account book. Jimmy Dingwell is heard singing off* R. *He appears at the window and speaks through it.*

DINGWELL. Good day, McDonald.
McDONALD. Ah, Jimmy Dingwell. Come in. (*Dingwell enters* U.) An' what have ye been up to now with yer murderous instincts —be it shape, hogs or kittle?
DINGWELL. That old brindle cow of the widder McDougall—she didn't freshen this year, so I butchered her yisterday. What part of her would ye be likin'?

McDONALD. I don't know. I'll ask the woman. (*He opens the staircase door and thumps on one of the stairs.*)
DINGWELL. Be Maggie back with ye?
McDONALD. Nay, she's home to Southport. She didn't like it here none. It's me daughter Belinda's runnin' the house now.
DINGWELL. Oh, the dummy!
McDONALD. I said me daughter.
DINGWELL. No offense, man. (*Glancing at the cradle.*) Ye niver found out, did ye, McDonald, who the father was?
McDONALD. (*Coming behind table to Dingwell.*) Dingwell, I'll thank ye to kape yer mind on the butcherin' business and don't overcharge me, then me and you'll remain friends, but not if ye poke yer nose in me private affairs.
DINGWELL. Still, I think ye should hear it. Yer not the man to take it layin' down—no more'n the doctor.
McDONALD. The doctor? And how does the gossip consarn him?
DINGWELL. Well, they do say the doctor and the dummy bein' so much togither—they're both young—and what kin ye expict?
McDONALD. (*Throwing book into drawer of table and slamming it shut.*) Well, I'll be damned! The finest man God iver let live—an' all the good he's done in the sittlement—up all day and night —summer an' winter—no journey too long, no weather too desprit —and gettin' no pay fer it. Who started that dirt?
DINGWELL. I dunno who started it, but there's a lot helpin' it on. Last night at Pocket's store—and today around with me mate—
McDONALD. Mrs. McKee, I'll warrant. By the Godfrey, I'd like to boot her backside and hoist her as high as the Planet Jupiter! The bitch! Niver had no children of her own—and if she had, they'd starve fer all they'd find under that flat chest of hers!
DINGWELL. I ain't sayin' yes, and I ain't sayin' no!
McDONALD. God damn that nose of hers—'tis iverywhere it don't belong. If I meet her in the village, I'll rub it on the base of the first lamp post.
DINGWELL. You do, and I'll hold her feet! I've got a score of me own I'd like to sittle with that old hen. And now would ye be likin' a bit of beef?
McDONALD. Drive yer wagon up to the fince. I'll jine ye in a jeffy. (*Dingwell exits U. Belinda enters from upstairs with Johnny Belinda in her arms, crosses to cradle below table and places baby in it.*) Now thin, let's git the hang of this. (*He raps the table for*

Belinda's attention. She turns at the cradle to look. He points off L. after Dingwell, then spells out laboriously on his R. hand, quoting the letters as he makes them.) B-U-C-H-E-R. Now that's an awful tax on me mintal faculties. *(Belinda signs and McDonald interprets—"You forgot the 'T.'")* All right, the "T" *. Howiver ye spell it, 'tis the boocher. Would ye be wantin' anythin' *? (* *Signed.* * *This articulated clearly. Belinda signs: "What has he got?")* He's got a cow. * (* *Signed. Belinda signs: "Is it dead?")* Of course she's dead. How the hell would you be atin' her if she ain't dead? *(Belinda makes sign for: "I'm laughing at you.")* Stop yer laffin' now! What would ye be likin'? * (* *Articulated clearly. Belinda makes a sign for eating soup.)* I suppose ye want a bone for some soup for the baby. Anything else? * (* *Articulated clearly. Belinda spells out: B-A-K-E.)* "B-A-K-E." Oh, it's a roast ye want. I'll pick out a bit of liver for meself. *(He starts for the door U. and meets Dr. Jack coming in.)*

DR. JACK. Hello, Mac. Want any meat? Dingwell's in the yard. *(Belinda moves to L. of table.)*

McDONALD. Jest goin' ter see him. Bring yerself to anchor. I'll be back in a minute. *(McDonald exits.)*

DR. JACK. *(Touching Belinda fondly, he deposits his bag in McDonald's chair.)* Hello! How's the big man this afternoon? *(He goes to cradle, the head of which is downstage.)* Hello, Johnny Belinda, you cute little rascal! You almost missed the boat, do you know that? *(He moves to R. of head of cradle and claps his hands, then passing below cradle claps his hands on L. side of it. Belinda taps chair L. of table to attract his attention and signs: "Hearing?")*

DR. JACK. His hearing? *(Moving below table to Belinda.)* Fine! Nothing wrong with his hearing, thank Heaven! Perfect! * (* *Signed. Belinda makes sign for "pleasure." He takes a pair of miniature mittens from her work basket.)* What's this? Mittens for Johnny Belinda!

McDONALD. *(Returning. Door U. C.)* Here's your cow! *(Brings in meat and places it on sink. Belinda takes minature cap from basket.)*

DR. JACK. A tam o' shanter! Look at the size of it!

McDONALD. And a nice bone to make some soup fer little Johnny Belinda. *(He moves down to cradle. Belinda sees McDonald moving to cradle with his soiled hands and crosses quickly to him,*

48

taking his hands in her fingers and leading him to the sink, where she pumps some water and makes him wash.)

DR. JACK. Let that be a lesson to you. We're sanitary around here.

McDONALD. Since you've been after her, I can't call me soul me own. *(Belinda picks up the meat, takes it into pantry; brings out a broom and goes out on the storm porch* U. *to sweep it. McDonald wipes his hands on the roller towel. Dr. Jack sits in chair back of table.)*

DR. JACK. How are you getting along, Mac?

McDONALD. Ah, man dear! Happy as bugs in a rug.

DR. JACK. I hope you haven't pestered her any more as to who the father is. *(Belinda is sweeping the porch.)*

McDONALD. Nay. Last time I mentioned it, she gave me such a curious look, I couldn't tell whether she was defyin' me to lay hands on her or warning me to hold me tongue. At any rate tis forgotten. *(Belinda moves off the porch. McDonald comes* D. *to cradle.)* Ain't he handsome, now?

DR. JACK. He's a McDonald all right.

McDONALD. He is that! Ah, ye little rascal! Yer a McDonald—and let no man tell ye nay. *(He moves toward shelf for pipe.)* Doctor—I want to thank ye fer takin' care of that payment for Pocket. *(He lights pipe.)*

DR. JACK. Not at all, Mac—glad to help out.

McDONALD. He wasn't a bit friendly when I showed up with the money.

DR. JACK. Of course not. You've got a good farm here and he'd like to own it. We've got to get it all paid off.

McDONALD. Man dear, you're expictin' the impossible.

DR. JACK. *(He rises and crosses below table and round* L. *of it, circling it and back to chair back of table.)* Oh, no, Mac. I've written to Montreal to see if there are any vacancies in the hospital. I'd like to get my old job back—for the winter anyway.

McDONALD. What—give up yer practice here?

DR. JACK. I've got no practice. Everyone with a pain or ache runs down to Dr. McLaughlin at Southport. I haven't had a patient for a month.

McDONALD. I see.

DR. JACK. I don't understand it. I've been fairly successful curing peoples' ills. I don't overcharge.

McDONALD. From all I hear you niver sind a bill.

DR. JACK. However—McLaughlin's all right—a little antiquated, but conscientious. Point is I've got to make some money. Goin' to pay off all your debts—get you a mowing machine and other things the farm needs. I can only do that in Montreal.

McDONALD. What prompts you to do all this fer me?

DR. JACK. I'm not doing it for you, you old so-and-so,—it's for your daughter and that fine youngster of hers.

McDONALD. (*Taking a step to him.*) Well, Doctor, I've heard there's a good deal of gossip in the sittlement—that you're not a God-fearin' man—'d rather keep your nose in a book or go fishin' than attind meetin' on Sunday. But me thinks yer a damn sight better Christian than most.

DR. JACK. Thank you, Mac.

McDONALD. And I'll be sorry to see you go. (*Belinda re-enters and replaces broom in pantry, L.*)

DR. JACK. I'll be sorry to leave.

McDONALD. (*He makes for the pantry to get the demijohn.*) Would ye be likin' a dish? (*Belinda comes out of pantry, takes her work-basket from table and goes to R. end of sofa, where she sits, unravelling wool.*)

DR. JACK. A dish! Look in my bag—I've brought you a real drink. It's a wonder you've got any insides left with your "dishes."

McDONALD. (*He takes a bottle of Scotch whiskey from Dr. Jack's bag.*) Scotch! Tis a long time since I rolled me tongue over anythin' as good as that! (*They have a drink and McDonald smacks his lips.*)

DR. JACK. How are you getting along with the sign language?

McDONALD. I find me spillin' kind o' rusty. She started coddin' me today because I forgot the "T" *. (*Making symbol.*) in "boocher." But 'tis amazin' what ye've taught her. (*Belinda is looking at him.*) Look man, how she reads me lips: "Man" *. (* *Clearly articulated. Belinda makes the sign.*) "Woman" *. (* *Clearly articulated. Belinda makes the sign.*) "Baby" *. (* *Clearly articulated. Belinda makes the sign.*) Quick as a flash, ain't she?

DR. JACK. Watch this, Mac: Belinda!—Who—is—the—most—beautiful—girl—in—the—world?" (*Clearly articulated. Belinda humorously and delicately thumbs her nose at him.*) That's one I never taught her.

McDONALD. (*Raising his glass.*) Well, man, here's to her Majesty!
DR. JACK. (*Springing to his feet and toasting.*) The Queen! God bless her. (*Locky McCormick appears in the doorway, U. and leans against left door jamb.*)
LOCKY. Hello, Mac!
McDONALD. (*Uncordial but polite.*) Oh, how be ye, McCormick?
LOCKY. Hello, Doctor!
DR. JACK. Good day—Locky! (*He moves to L. shielding Belinda from Locky's view.*)
LOCKY. I'm here to tell you, Mac, your sheep's in me grainfield an' it's just new seeded.
McDONALD. I'll have 'em out in a jeffy!
LOCKY. How's the youngster, McDonald?
McDONALD. He's not too bad, thank ye.
LOCKY. Do you mind if I have a look? I ain't niver seen him yit.
McDONALD. Take a look and wilcome. (*He takes glasses back to sink. Locky drops D. to cradle. He comes into Belinda's line of sight. She rises and looks anxiously across Dr. Jack to crib. Dr. Jack tries to restrain her from making any move which would arouse McDonald's suspicions.*)
LOCKY. Well now, by the Godfrey, that's a cute baby, an' no mistake! Well! Well! Hello, young man! (*Belinda rushes across and takes baby from crib and carries it upstairs. Locky follows Belinda with a surly glance, then rises and goes quickly to door, U.*) Drive out yer sheep, McDonald. If ye'd kape yer fince in dacent repair I'd not be botherin' ye. (*He exits. There is a tense pause.*)
McDONALD. (*Moving to back of table.*) Did you see that?
DR. JACK. See what, Mac? (*Moving to table and averting his eyes.*)
McDONALD. (*He crosses to table.*) The guilty look on McCormick's face whin she confronted him? An' whin I spoke to 'im, he could nay look me in the eye. By God, Doctor, I can tell by the look in yer own eye, the same thought is in yer mind! D'ye think 'twas that bastard what done it?
DR. JACK. Mac! I thought you'd forgotten all that.
McDONALD. (*Pacing up and down, R. C.*) An' why not? In an' out of the mill at all hours, now that I think of it. Have her down. I want to ask her a few questions, once an' fer all!

DR. JACK. Man! What good will that do?

McDONALD. I'll get some slape, for one thing. I lie there night after night, tryin' to figure the thing out—Me own daughter here in me own house! An' the whole sittlemint gossipin' like I had no guts to protect me own family. I'll sittle this matter now. (*Crossing to Dr. Jack who is* U. L. *of table.*)

DR. JACK. Mac! (*Barring his way.*)

McDONALD. If you don't call her, I will.

DR. JACK. (*Restraining him.*) No, Mac, I don't want Belinda upset.

McDONALD. Why, they're even sayin' that you are the father of Johnny Belinda.

DR. JACK. I!

McDONALD. That's why ye've got no practice—why the community's run out on ye! Are ye goin' to take that layin' down?

DR. JACK. Why, that's absurd, and you know it.

McDONALD. Of course I know it. It's that Mrs. McKee an' the rest. But now's the time to clean iverything up. It's McCormick—I'm dead certain of it. (*Moving away to* R. C.)

DR. JACK. Mac—I know who the man is. (*McDonald turns to him sharply.*) Belinda has told me. And I advised her to say nothing to anyone about it, not even you.

McDONALD. (*Crossing over to Dr. Jack and placing hands on his shoulders.*) It is McCormick! Am I right?

DR. JACK. Yes. You're right.

McDONALD. I knew it! Why, the son of a bitch! I'll blow his guts out! (*He rushes for shotgun which hangs above the* U. *door, and reaches for it.*)

DR. JACK. (*He goes quickly and holds his arms, restraining him.*) Mac, I don't want you to cause any trouble! I'll take care of the boy and Belinda too.—Wait a minute, Mac, what good will any of that do?

McDONALD. The bastard! I'll see daylight through him! (*He reaches again for the gun.*)

DR. JACK. (*Restraining him.*) I know you're a proud man, Mac—and I respect you for it—but there's nothing to be gained by violence—nor scandal either. It would be horrible for Belinda.—Mac, I want to marry her.

McDONALD. You?

DR. JACK. Yes, and I'd rather she were spared all this. Since the

community thinks I'm the father—well, I'll be the father and a mighty proud one too. (*Slowly McDonald ceases his struggle to get the gun.*)
McDONALD. Be you in earnest, man?
DR. JACK. I was never more in earnest. That's another reason why I want to go to Montreal to make some money. (*He moves D. to McDonald's left arm.*) Now, let's forget it, shall we?
McDONALD. All right, man. Have it yer own way. (*Belinda enters from stairs. She is slightly apprehensive of what she may find, then seeing their manner, and noting that Locky is not there, she signs to the doctor: "Is everything all right?"*) What's that she's sayin'?
DR. JACK. She's asking if everything is all right.
McDONALD. (*He moves to her and takes her by the arms.*) Yes, child—everything is quite all right now. (*He kisses her on the forehead. He is so moved that he can hardly refrain from crying, and he covers this by dabbing his eyes with a little self-conscious chuckle.*) Well, I think I'll git at that fince. (*He picks up a pail of nails and goes out to the porch. There is a low roll of thunder.*) There's a storm coming up. (*He exits. Belinda stands where he has kissed her. She looks at the doctor and signs: "What did you tell my father?"*)
DR. JACK. "What was I telling your father?" I was telling him what a fine girl you are, and how pleased I am with the progress * you are making with your lessons *. (*These words signed *. Belinda shakes her head.*) But I was! Now, get your books! Your books! (*Belinda reluctantly goes to shelf over R. and takes two copy-books —a writing book and an arithmetic one. Doctor seats himself at back of table. As Belinda comes back to table, a flurry of wind churns dust and leaves up in the porch. She goes up and closes the door. A Lightning Flash comes outside window. She runs to the window eagerly and signs: "Lightning!"*) Yes—Lightning. (*Thunder. She comes to the table and puts her hand on it, waiting for the vibration of the thunder. When it has come, she signs: "Thunder."*) Yes—and thunder, too. (*She signs: "I love thunderstorms."*) Oh, you love thunderstorms, do you? Well, I don't. (*Lightning Flash. She signs: "Fire."*) Fire! (*She puts her hand on table for vibration. Thunder. It comes. She signs: "Music."*) Music? Oh, yes —— That's your music when the table shakes! Well, never mind the thunderstorm! Your homework. (* *Signed.*

She crosses and sits L. *of table with a slight pout. Dr. Jack opens the writing book and reads.*) "I love my baby the world is beautiful." —I love my baby—period. The world is beautiful—period. Always a period at the end of a sentence, Belinda. (*With a face she takes the pencil and makes exaggerated periods on the book. She thanks him with a nod.*) Very well written, though. (*Flash of Lightning. She puts her hand on the table—a crash comes—after a count of three. She loves the vibration. He smiles at her tolerantly.*) Now your arithmetic. (*He takes the other copy-book. Belinda makes a wry face.*) What's this? * What's this? * (*Signed *.*) Seven times two are how many? (*She shakes her head.*) Look, Belinda—seven times two are the same as two times seven. Count them. (*He puts up his two hands with fingers extended. Rapidly with her finger she tells off his fingers up to ten. Then she has difficulty and with concentration she gets—eleven—twelve—thirteen—fourteen—Belinda takes a pencil and writes* 14, *making a face at him.*) Fourteen —Correct! And don't make such faces! They're terrible. (*She grins.*) Three times four are twelve—Four times four are sixteen —Belinda, five times— (*She gets impatient and fussily closes the book and pushes it away.*) Oh, you don't like work! (*She signs: "Some work."*) Some work? (*She signs: "I like signs."*) Oh, you like the signs, do you? Well you just come here and sign "Comin' Through the Rye" for me. (*He takes her hand and leads her to* U. L. *He prepares to show her the signs. But she puts down his hands and signs: "I know it."*) Oh, you know it, do you? Well, let * me * see *! (* *Signed. She nods and motions him to his chair. She now signs, "Comin' Through the Rye" while he repeats:*) "If a body—meet a body Comin' through the Rye— If a body kiss a body—Need a body cry? Every Lassie has her *laddie*— Not one they say have I! Y-e-t all the boys they smile at me Comin' through the Rye. * (*Applauding her.*) Splendid, Belinda. You *have* worked, haven't you? (*A terrific crash and a blinding flash together.*) My God! That was close! (*Belinda runs to the window. The rain descends in torrents.*) Belinda! Come away from that window! (*Belinda signs: "I'm not afraid."*) You're not afraid? Well, you should be. Come, come, dear. I want you to sit here. (*He seats Belinda at the back of the table. He sits at* L. *of it.*) I want to try some oral * work. (* *Signed. Belinda copies the sign, not understanding it.*) Speaking! * (*She grasps this and makes*

54

*the sign for "Talking," clapping her hands lightly for intense pleasure.) Now, we'll take this word. (He writes on a piece of paper, "John-ny.") "Johnny." (She is pleased and blows a kiss to the baby in the cradle.) Now, look—two * syllables *. (* Signed. She understands.) Now, look—(He pronounces "J-o-h-n" very broadly with movement of lips. She tries to speak it. Her lips move but no sound comes.) Put your hand on my throat. (He places her hand on his throat and pronounces it again.) J-o-h-n. (She puts her right hand on her own throat, keeping her left on his as he speaks.) J-o-h-n. (She tries to repeat after him. Her lips move but no sound comes, and pathetically she drops her hands. He puts her hand back on his throat again.) Now—watch my lips. (She feels her own throat again.) J-o-h-n—n-y. (She tries to say it but no sound comes. Floyd McGuiggan enters the U. Door hurriedly.)*

FLOYD. Dr. Jack!

DR. JACK. What is it, Floyd?

FLOYD. There's been an accident!

DR. JACK. What's happened?

FLOYD. Black McDonald!

DR. JACK. What about him?

FLOYD. He's been killed!

DR. JACK. Killed?

FLOYD. Struck by lightning. He was fixing Locky's fince. There was a bunch of us there, and we seen it happen. It fair blinded us. Then there was McDonald layin' on the ground—his clothes smokin' like he'd been raked from a fire.

DR. JACK. Where is he?

FLOYD. They're bringing him in. (*Exits.*)

DR. JACK. (*Going to Belinda and signing *.*) Belinda, your father is hurt—the lightning. (*She tries to go, but he restrains her. Locky and McPhearson carry in the body of McDonald. Floyd comes first and clears the way for them to carry it D. L. C. Stella comes in and goes to Belinda R., and comforts her. Locky, having deposited the body, goes up to the rear and stands by the sink. McPhearson stands over R., Floyd L. of table. Dr. Jack goes to the body and examines it. He sees McDonald is dead and rises slowly. Belinda goes quickly to the body and looks at the closed eyes. The Doctor gives way for her, so he is on her R. She turns to him and makes the sign for "Dead?" He nods his head. She raises McDonald's* *right hand to her lips and places it gently on his breast. She looks upward and signs the Lord's Prayer, the Doctor repeating the words.*) Our Father, Who art in Heaven, hallowed be Thy name, Thy Kingdom come, Thy will be done on Earth as it is in Heaven. Give us this day our daily bread and forgive us our trespasses as we forgives those who trespass against us. Lead us not into temptation but deliver us from Evil, for Thine is the power and the glory forever. Amen. (*Then as the storm clears and the sun begins to shine again, Belinda signs: "Goodnight, father." Dr. Jack interpreting.*) Goodnight, father. (*Fade out.*)

CURTAIN

END OF SECOND ACT

ACT THREE

Scene 1

The Kitchen.
Belinda is by the stove. She pours some warm water into a saucepan, in which are the baby's bottles. Stella, in winter clothes, comes in through U. *door to behind the table, raps on the table.*

STELLA. Hello, Dummy! (*She has a paper bag with knitted garments in it.*) See, what I brought for the baby! * (*Clearly articulated * as she holds up the garment. Belinda moves to her with the sign for "Beautiful!" Then she makes signs: "Did you make it?"*) Yes—I made it. (*She goes to the cradle and dangles the garment before the baby.*) See, Johnny Belinda! See what I made for you!— Isn't he wonderful? * May I pick him up? * (* *Clearly articulated. Belinda nods. Stella picks up the baby and holds him in her arms at* R. *of cradle, singing a little jingle to him.*) Look at him smile! He likes music *. (* *Clearly articulated *. Belinda is pleased. She takes the baby, holds it in her arms, petting it, then leans down and kisses it, then returns it to the crib as Dr. Jack enters. He wears his fur coat and removes his cap.*) Oh —— Dr. Jack. (*Belinda picks up the garment Stella has knitted for the baby, indicates the baby in the crib and points to Stella. The doctor understands.*)
DR. JACK. Did you make that for the baby Stella?
STELLA. Yes, sir. Winter and all.
DR. JACK. No prospects of your own yet?
STELLA. No, sir; more's the pity. Goodbye, Dummy. (*Belinda signs: "I like this very much."*) What's she sayin'?
DR. JACK. She says she likes it very much.
STELLA. You're more'n welcome. Good day, Doctor. (*Stella exits* U.)
DR. JACK. Good day, Stella. (*Belinda starts to unbutton his fur coat.*) I can't stay, Belinda. I haven't much time *. (* *Signed.*

Belinda signs: "*A few minutes.*") Well—just a very few minutes. (*He allows Belinda to take his coat and cap and hang them up. He writes on his pad of paper. She comes back from the coat pegs and looks over his shoulder.*) Belinda, if the baby is ever sick, send for Dr. McLaughlin at Southport *. (*All this very clearly articulated * so that Belinda can read his lips and the name and place of the doctor, pointing to the pad where he has written them. Belinda signs: "I shall send for you."*) I'm going away. I must catch a train in forty minutes. (*Belinda signs: "Why?"*) Because I must make some money *. (* *Signed. Belinda signs: "Where are you going?"*) Long * travel * —on the boat * —on the train * a thousand * miles *. (* *Signed.*) Montreal. (*She does not understand this, so he spells it with the alphabet. Still she doesn't understand. He opens the map and shows her.*) Here—on the map. Montreal. (*She signs: "When will you come back?"*) I'll be back for Christmas *. (* *Signed.*) Come—we'll mark it on the calendar. (*He crosses to the calendar, takes it off the wall and sits at table. She takes a chair beside him. He rings a date on the calendar with his pencil.*) There—December 25th—in six weeks. (*She signs: "Be careful."*) Yes,—I'll be careful. (*She signs: "I shall die if harm comes to you."*) You—will die if harm comes to me? No harm will come, dear. (*She signs: "I love you."*) You love me? And I love you. Belinda—what does marriage mean to you? (*Very tenderly he says this as if promising great happiness for them. She signs, he translates.*) "I—have—seen—a young—man—and a young—woman—come smiling from—the church—and drive away—and live together—under one roof—and children come—and laughter —but always they—are together—in joy and sadness—in work—and play—until they—are old. That is marriage—to me." And to me, too, Belinda. Will you marry me? (*Her arms go around his neck and their lips meet.*) Then at Christmas we will be married. * (*A kiss. He glances at his wrist watch. She covers it with her hand.*) Yes—now I must go —— (*He crosses to the cradle, picking up his map as he does so, from table.*) Goodbye, Johnny Belinda. You'll be calling me 'pop' one of these days. We'll have a Christmas Tree * and presents * for you * and your mother *. (* *Signed.*) Take good care of her while I am away. (*He goes to Belinda, who is holding his coat, puts it on, takes his cap from the peg, turns to Belinda, who signs: "Don't forget me."*) I can't forget you. You are in my mind and my heart always. Goodbye, dear. (*He kisses* her again and goes. She stands in the porch watching him go, and waves to him through the window as he retreats. Belinda closes the door, stands by it for a moment, then goes happily to the cradle, blows kiss to the baby. Feels that he needs another cover. She goes upstairs, closing the door behind her. Very shortly afterwards, Mrs. McKee and Mrs. Lutz are seen passing the kitchen window. A few paces behind comes Rev. Tidmarsh. Mrs. McKee peers through the window into room. She knocks sharply, then opens the door and enters, followed by Mrs. Lutz.)

MRS. McKEE. No use knocking. She couldn't hear us anyway. She don't seem to be at home. (*She goes straight to the door* D. L.)

MRS. LUTZ. (*She takes off her gloves and hangs up her fur coat to* L. *of door on pegs.*) She may be at the mill or gone to the village. (*Mrs. McKee has peered into room* D. L.)

TIDMARSH. (*Enters. He, too, has his fur coat on.*) I just saw the doctor drive away. (*Mrs. Lutz has dropped* R. *to the stove to warm her hands and glances at the baby.*)

MRS. McKEE. I thought he left on the mornin' train.

MRS. LUTZ. Perhaps she went to see him off.

MRS. McKEE. And I did want the Riverend to see fer himself the kind of immoral creature she is. You kin tell by the look of her. Let me take your coat, your Riverence. (*She takes Tidmarsh's coat and hangs it up, hanging her own up afterwards.*)

MRS. LUTZ. Strange ye niver met her, yer Riverence.

TIDMARSH. (*Dropping* D. R. *to Mrs. Lutz.*) Not so strange, Mrs. Lutz. The one time I called on Black McDonald and chided him for not attending church and bringing his daughter along, he ordered me off the place. This would be her child, I suppose. (*Adjusting his pince-nez.*)

MRS. LUTZ. Aye—and see how she neglicts him. Off gaddin' aboot an' leaving the brat here to burn up if the place took afire. (*Belinda hurries in from upstairs with a baby's blanket. She is suprised to see them, but very pleased—thinking they are paying a social call. She signs: "I am pleased to meet you all."*) Now, what might all that mean?

MRS. McKEE. Some of the signs the doctor's been teachin' her, nay doot. (*Belinda draws over McDonald's chair from* U. R. *to* T. *of table for Mrs. Lutz who goes to it. She indicates chair back of table for Mrs. McKee, who takes it. Then she motions Tidmarsh to the chair* L. *of table. He sits. She stands between him and Mrs. Mc-*

Kee and signs: "Seeing you all here gives me great pleasure." It has a little flicking motion to the breast.) I tremble to think what that may signify. The immodesty of the creature! (*Belinda moves to stove behind Mrs. McKee.*) No wonder the boys of the sittlemint flock around the mill. Wonder is she wasn't in trouble sooner. (*Belinda puts blanket on cradle, then pours tea in the pot and covers the leaves with boiling water, then crosses to pantry. She comes out with a small tray on which are three cups, three saucers, sugar bowl and creamer and three spoons.*)

TIDMARSH. One can hardly believe it of the doctor. (*Mrs. McKee and Tidmarsh remove the dishes and spoons from the tray, and Belinda takes the tray away.*)

MRS. McKEE. And what's so hard to believe aboot it? A man who never wint to church—who's lavin' the country without fulfilling his obligations to this girl an' her offspring, or even payin' his bills.

MRS. LUTZ. He left owin' Pocket fer a month's groceries. Even Stella didn't get her wages. But she swears he'll pay her.

MRS. McKEE. Stella was always a bit soft in the head. (*Belinda places cake and knife on table, slicing the cake four times—then returns to stove.*)

MRS. LUTZ. Look now, the airs of her! As if presidin' at a church social! I hate to accept anythin' she touches.

TIDMARSH. We mustn't offend the creature. (*Belinda pours more water in teapot.*)

MRS. McKEE. You notice the manner of her, yer Riverence, not a bit humiliated at finding herself among respectable people.

MRS. LUTZ. No moral sinse whatever. I hope we won't be contaminated eatin' her cake.

TIDMARSH. (*Testing the cake.*) 'Tis right good. I'll take a whole piece. (*Belinda crosses with tea pot to table, then crosses to pantry for three plates and returns, placing them around table; then returns to crib, tucks blanket around baby.*)

MRS. McKEE. Now to come to the point, yer Riverence. The Ladies Aid is much concerned as to what's to become of this girl and her fatherless brat.

TIDMARSH. Ah, 'tis a sad case an' no mistake.

MRS. McKEE. The Dummy kin take care of hersilf nay doot; 'tis the baby we're thinkin' aboot. Brought up with no church no school, not even a mither it kin talk to, or learn it to say its prayers.

MRS. LUTZ. Yer fergitten, Mrs. McKee, Pocket's threatenin' to git a judgment fer the amount of McDonald's bill an' seize the farm.

MRS. McKEE. True indade. They'll be on the road. (*Belinda comes back to table.*)

MRS. LUTZ. The dummy's a right smart cook. Do ye mind the cake she made for the Sunday School picnic, Mrs. McKee?

MRS. McKEE. I do. It was a lemon layer, Mrs. Johnstone at the bridge bought it at auction fer twinty-five cints—that would be Mrs. Willie Arthur Johnstone. —— (*Without enthusiasm.*) A good cake. (*She makes a face.*) Too much soda.

TIDMARSH. I'm thinkin' we might place her as a cook.

MRS. McKEE. That won't be easy, yer Riverence on account of her morals. I wouldn't want her in *my* kitchen with all the byes of the neighborhood astride of the back fince. Here's Stella and Locky now. (*She goes and opens door, U.—to Stella.*) I was wonderin' why you and Locky was late. I said we'd be here at four.

STELLA. I was here earlier. Hello, Dummy. Hello, Mrs. Lutz. Good day, yer Riverence. (*Locky enters from porch and throws off his coat.*)

TIDMARSH. Well, Locky me bye, gittin' yer winter wood in? (*Locky hangs his coat and cap on peg. Belinda stands by stove, looking puzzled.*)

LOCKY. Yarded out ten cord this mornin'.

TIDMARSH. Don't forget, I'll be needin' about three cord meself, cut to firewood length. (*Locky sits down on sofa beside Stella. Belinda goes into pantry, gets cup, saucer, plate, returns to stove, fills cup for Stella.*)

LOCKY. I'll not let ye freeze, yer Riverence.

MRS. McKEE. I was just comin' to the matter of the baby, Locky. Ye see, yer Riverence, it was Locky what brought to our attention this unfortunate situation.

TIDMARSH. Ah, the good Samaratin! (*Belinda crosses to Stella with cup.*)

MRS. McKEE. As he pointed out, it would be much better for the brat if we could find some good family where we could place 'im. Church mimbers and all that. (*Belinda puts piece of cake from table on plate and takes it to Stella.*)

TIDMARSH. Ah yes, that would be the pure thing.

MRS. McKEE. Adopt him, ye twig?

TIDMARSH. Yes, yes. Another dish o' tea? (*Lifts his cup toward Belinda who fills it from the pot on stove.*)

MRS. McKEE. Now, yer riverence, Stella and Locky have no children of their own, poor dears, an' they'd be willin' to adopt the bye, for charity's sake, ye understand. Mrs. Lutz, the list. (*Belinda brings cup to Tidmarsh. She has deliberately avoided giving Locky any tea or cake, and has kept as far away from him as possible, and now goes to the crib as if to guard it and Johnny Belinda as long as Locky is in the room. Mrs. Lutz takes a paper from her bag.*) I have a pertition yer Riverence. All the good ladies in the village—askin' kin this be done?

TIDMARSH. An' what is it ye wish me to do?

MRS. McKEE. Apply to the proper authorities an' fix it so Stella and Locky kin adopt the bye.

TIDMARSH. Ye wish to adopt the bye, Locky?

LOCKY. Aye! I'd give a deal fer a bye the likes of him.

TIDMARSH. Stella —— (*Locky nudges Stella.*)

STELLA. Oh yes, yer Riverence. (*Belinda brings the baby jacket and shows it to Mrs. McKee, indicating Stella.*)

MRS. LUTZ. Did you make that for the baby, Stella?

STELLA. Yes, Mrs. Lutz. (*Belinda crosses to Stella and kisses her.*)

MRS. McKEE. Stella, don't let her kiss ye! The brazen hussy! Kissin' a dacent woman! (*Belinda returns to the crib to guard it.*)

TIDMARSH. (*Rising.*) Well, I'll see what kin be done.

MRS. McKEE. (*Rising.*) That's a good job started.

MRS. LUTZ. (*Crosses to crib, and looks down at Johnny Belinda.*) Well, little man, ye'll have a good home from this on.

MRS. McKEE. (*Crossing to crib for a look at the baby herself.*) An' a faather he kin be proud of. Congratulations, Locky!

LOCKY. (*Getting his cap.*) Much obliged to you, Mrs. McKee. (*Tidmarsh dropping down L.*)

MRS. McKEE. Oh, dear! He's the dead spittin' image of her. Look at the eyes, will ye. Full of the old nick. Locky, ye'll have yer hands full! (*Mrs. Lutz hands Mrs. McKee her coat. Tidmarsh crosses to crib.*)

LOCKY. Don't worry aboot that, woman, I'll learn him or blister his bottom!

MRS. LUTZ. Now, Locky, don't be too hard on 'im. Ye can't be blamin' him fer his mither's sins.

MRS. McKEE. Mrs. Lutz, yer fergettin' yer Bible: "Spare the rod an' spoil the child." Locky's just the father fer him. (*Belinda shows Tidmarsh baby sweater.*)

TIDMARSH. (*Takes Belinda's hand and pats the back of it.*) We must timper the winds to the shorn lamb.

MRS. McKEE. (*At Tidmarsh's* L.) She can't hear a word ye're sayin', yer riverence.

TIDMARSH. Niverthelss, we must be charitable. Remember "not a sparrow falleth." I shall consider it me Christian dooty to look after these two unfortunates. The child will fare well with Stella and Locky. And we must find a good home for this poor sinner. (*Moving to table.*) I shall pray for her. I shall labor that she may be washed in the blood of the lamb, that she may sin no more, and inherit eternal life. (*Takes a bit of cake, and puts it in his mouth as he moves to door.*) That's excellent cake! (*They all leave except Stella who lingers by the table and as soon as the others are gone she starts collecting the soiled cups and saucers and plates for Belinda to save her the trouble. But Belinda goes quickly to her, gently stops her, and urges her to the door, where she kisses her again for the sweater, gives her a pat on the shoulder and sends her after the others. Stella, with a smile, waves goodby to her, and exits.*)

CURTAIN

ACT THREE

Scene 2

The Kitchen.
Belinda pours buttermilk from a churn into a bucket, then rinses the churn with water from the pump at the sink. Stella is working the butter in a big wooden bowl. Belinda comes to Stella to take bowl.

STELLA. Oh, I'll finish the butter. (*Belinda smiles—slips her feet into overshoes, puts on cap and mackinaw and mittens. Stella stops her.*) Dummy, kin I take the baby home with me? (* *Clearly articulated, pointing. Belinda shakes her head, "No."*) Please, Dummy,—just a little while? (*Belinda gets a cake from the pantry and offers it to Stella, putting it on table.*) For me? Oh, Dummy, I couldn't take it. Dummy, please let me take the baby home with me? *(Belinda shakes her head, "No," picks up bucket and exits, is seen passing window U. R. Stella watches Belinda, crosses to crib and looking at baby.)* For gosh shakes, I wish I'd never got into this! *(Locky enters from the direction opposite that taken by Belinda and shuts the door.)*

LOCKY. What's kapin' ye, girl?

STELLA. Oh, Locky, ye scared me!

LOCKY. What be ye hangin' around here for? *(Stella crosses below table to L. chair.)*

STELLA. I was helpin' the Dummy with the butter. She just done finished churnin'.

LOCKY. Where's she now?

STELLA. Gone round to the barn with the buttermilk fer the pigs. *(Locky crosses to crib and looks at baby.)*

LOCKY. Well, Cap'n, I'm yer pa now, an' this is yer ma. I've an awful cravin' to dangle the little bugger on me knee. *(Moves to L. of sink, lookes off R. through window.)* Look spry, woman. Fetch 'im along.

STELLA. Locky, we can't just take him like this.

LOCKY. What are ye talkin' aboot? *(Back of table.)* He's ourn—been give to us, all legal and proper. There's the papers to prove it.

STELLA. I know, but it's so cruel to the Dummy.

LOCKY. Cruel, me eye! She's dumb, ye ninny. It makes no more difference to her than weanin' a calf from a cow. Come on! I want to get to the village an' buy what we'll be nadin' fer him.

STELLA. But I've a dreadful feelin' somethin' will happen.

LOCKY. What kin happen? If the Dummy kicks up a fuss, or comes on the place, I'll have her bound over to kape the peace! The law's on our side, woman. Now stop ye blitherin' an' fitch 'im along!

STELLA. *(Rising and facing him.)* Locky, I ain't goin' to do it!

LOCKY. After we wint to all this trouble? Now, be reasonable, Stella. He's the makin' of a fine, sturdy lad. He'll hilp me with the work whin he's growd. A man kin starve on one of those here faarms without help. Look at Black McDonald, a lifetime o' tile, an' he nay could pay his bills.

STELLA. 'Tis not the work I'm afeared of. I'll help!

LOCKY. 'Tis the bye I want.
STELLA. (*Moving down* L. *to end of sofa.*) Locky, we must give him up!
LOCKY. What's that?
STELLA. I ain't slept a wink since he's been gived to us. We're mean, Locky. We're mean to the Dummy. Ye think she has no feelin's ye should see her with the baby. We can't take 'im, Locky. She's his mither.
LOCKY. His mither! Well, let me tell you somethin'. I'm his faather!
STELLA. What!
LOCKY. His faather, I'm tellin' ye! He's as much mine as hers! (*Stella sinks to couch and cries.*)
STELLA. Oh, Locky! I told ye to kape away from her.
LOCKY. (*Moving behind table to* R. *of it.*) Ah! What be ye cryin' aboot? 'Tis all over an' in the past. An fortunate it is, it happened. A man wants children. You can't give me none, that's sartin'. An' I want him. Somethin' here wants him. An' by the Godfrey I'll have him! (*He pounds the table. Belinda re-enters. Senses the situation. Stella seizes her coat from the sofa and runs out. Belinda goes quickly to the crib and takes the baby, running with him into the room* D. L. *Locky hesitates a moment* R. *of table, then crosses to door* D. L. *as Belinda re-enters, closes the door behind her and stands defiantly with her hand on the doorknob. She's still wearing her boots but has thrown off mackinaw and cap.*) Now, hear this, Dummy, that boy is mine! As much mine as yer own, an' I'm takin' him to live with me. You twig what I mane? Whether ye do or nay, yer to kape off my faarm, kape yer distance! An' now I'll be takin' him. (*Belinda tightens her grip on the doorknob.*) Now, oot of me way, Dummy, afore I hurt ye. (*She pushes him away.*) Oh, full of fight—be ye! Well, we'll see aboot that. . . . (*He slaps her face, and as she still pushes him away, he seizes her by one arm and yanking her away from the door gives her a vicious uppercut on the chin and knocks her out. She falls in a heap on the floor. He enters the room after the baby. Belinda slowly comes to, realizes what is happening, and looks around for help. Sees gun over door, quickly gets it down, sees it's not loaded, pulls down a whole box of shells, spilling them right and left, slips two into the gun and exits into the room after Locky.*)

LOCKY. (*Offstage—yelling.*) Dummy, stop! Don't shoot! (A SHOT IS HEARD. *A few moments later Belinda comes from the room, the baby safely in her arms.*)

CURTAIN

ACT THREE

SCENE 3

The Courtroom. A preliminary hearing.
The Judge in his black robes and white wig presides. On the wall back of him hangs a picture of Queen Victoria. Belinda is in the dock down R. McVail, the Defense Attorney, is examining Stella, who is on the stand, U. R. McKnight, the Public Prosecutor, is seated at his table in front of the spectators' benches, which contain—in the front row, Dr. Jack Davidson, Mrs. McKee, Mrs. Lutz and Tidmarsh—in the back row, Jimmy Dingwell and others, including the Matron. A Policeman in uniform stands guard.

McVAIL. Mrs. McCormick, you have heard the Crown contend that Belinda McDonald is an immoral woman, that Dr. Davidson was her lover and the father of her child, that she killed your husband in revenge because he had exposed her illicit relationship with the doctor?
STELLA. Yes, sir!
McVAIL. On the day your husband went to claim the child, you accompanied him, did you not?
STELLA. I did, sir!
McVAIL. Did he on that occasion say anything in regard to the child's parentage?
STELLA. Yes, sir!
McVAIL. Kindly tell the Court his exact words.
STELLA. He wanted me to take the baby, and I said, "We can't, it's cruel to the Dummy. She's his mither," and he said, "His mither! Well, let me tell you somethin', I'm his father!" (*Stir and sensation.*)

MRS. LUTZ. (*To Mrs. McKee, low voice.*) See? I told you you were wrong about the doctor.
McVAIL. (*Crossing to defense desk, L. C.*) Your witness, Mr. McKnight.
McKNIGHT. (*Rises; sits again.*) No questions. (*McVail looks surprised.*)
McVAIL. That's all; thank you, Mrs. McCormick. (*Stella leaves the stand and goes to row of seats, L.*) My lord, in your deliberations as to the guilt or innocence of Belinda McDonald, I ask you to remember the testimony of Dr. Davidson with regard to the deaf; that they live in a world apart, and are governed largely by instinct. Then try to remember that they inhabit a realm of silence, in which no sound, no song of bird, no tender word of friend or lover, parent or child can possibly penetrate. By the sign language—this system of ideographs—Dr. Davidson was able to instruct Belinda in certain simple fundamentals. He taught her the Ten Commandments—but something in her was stronger than the precept, "Thou shalt not kill." What she did was to obey an instinct older than the laws of man, an instinct without which life itself could not survive, the instinct of a female to protect her young, of a mother to protect and defend her child. I beg of you, to show mercy toward this girl so persecuted by fate and circumstance, to return the child to its mother, and spare her the cruelty and injustice of the charge of murder. (*He returns to his seat.*)
JUDGE. I should like to question this girl. Dr. Davidson, will you please interpret for her and me?
DR. JACK. Certainly, your lordship. (*He goes to Belinda.*) Face his lordship, Belinda. She must see your lips, my lord. Speak slowly, please.
JUDGE. Miss—McDonald—do—you—love—your—boy? (*Belinda breaks down, her shoulders shake as she weeps. Dr. Jack puts an arm around her shoulders and comforts her. Slowly she recovers. Dr. Jack offers his handkerchief and she dries her eyes.*)
DR. JACK. Answer, Belinda. (*Belinda signs—Dr. Jack interprets.*) "In—my—endless silence—life was meaningless—until he came. I fed him—I kept him warm—I could not sleep—if he fell ill— And when he smiled—my heart was filled with song—I love him —better than my life." (*She breaks down again, and again Dr. Jack comforts her.*)

JUDGE. Miss—McDonald —— Why—did—you—kill—Locky—McCormick? (*Belinda signs, Dr. Jack interprets.*)
DR. JACK. "He—hurt—me—I was—afraid—he—would—hurt—my—child."
JUDGE. That is all. You may sit down. Dr. Davidson, kindly return to your seat. (*Dr. Jack does so, and the Judge addresses the Crown Prosecutor.*) Mr. McKnight. (*McKnight rises.*) Mr. McKnight, I wish the Crown to take cognizance of certain facts not set forth in the indictment. Namely: McCormick betrayed this girl and went unpunished. Not content with this, he attempted to seize her child, legally, of course—but nonetheless maliciously. What she did was in defense of her person and her property.
McKNIGHT. My lord, the Crown expresses amazement at the turn the evidence has taken. Under the circumstances, the violation of Belinda's home was inexcusable and I recommend an investigation of the lax adoption laws, which made such a blunder possible.
JUDGE. I have made a note of it.
McKNIGHT. Had all the facts been known, the Crown would not have countenanced adoption of the child, or returned an indictment of murder. It is my business to prosecute and not to persecute, and I beg leave, my lord, to enter a plea of nolle prosequi. (*He resumes his seat down* L. C.)
JUDGE. Nevertheless, it is the duty of the Court to protect Society and to see to it that individuals refrain from taking the Law into their own hands. Dr. Davidson, since you have interested yourself in this girl, and the Crown refuses to prosecute—are you willing to assume responsibility for her actions in the future?
DR. JACK. (*Rising.*) I certainly am, my lord.
JUDGE. Then I order that the child be returned to its mother— (*Matron rises, goes out* U. L.) —and I parole the defendant in your care for a term of five years. Case dismissed!
CLERK. Her Majesty's Court stands adjourned sine die—God Save The Queen! (*Dr. Jack hurries to shake hands with the Judge and to thank him,—and to shake McVail's hand.*)
DR. JACK. (*Going to Belinda.*) * Belinda—you are free! (*Matron returns with baby, Belinda rushes from dock to take the baby lovingly in her arms.*)
BELINDA. (*Looking down at baby.*) JOHN—NY!

DR. JACK. (*Beside her, delighted.*) Belinda, you spoke his name!
BELINDA. (* *Signed.*) I—love—my baby!
DR. JACK. You love your baby? (*Belinda smiles and tenderly kisses the child. Dr. Jack speaks so that Belinda can read his lips.*) And—I—love—you—both—Belinda! (*She reaches a hand to him in affection and gratitude. He takes it, and they depart together.*)

CURTAIN

PROPERTY PLOT

Act I, Scene 1—Village Street

Fishing rod (Stella)
Creel, with fly book in it (Stella)
On Stage
Fence, with fish nets draped on it
Flower pots (3)
Off Right
Codfish (McGuffey)

Off Left
Tomato can (Floyd)
Small, hooked rug (Stella)
Rubber, hip boots (Dr. Jack)
Tray, with whiskey bottle & glass (Stella)

Act I, Scene 2—Grist Mill

On Stage
Sacks of grain (8 or 10)
Hopper, with on-off lever
Harness ⎫
Horse collars ⎬ (on pegs)
Coil of rope ⎪
Fish net ⎭
Notebook ⎫ (On nail)
Pencil ⎭
Hoes

Shovels
Rakes
Pickaxe
Broken chair
Bell
Off Left
Rod and creel (Dr. Jack)
Personal
Knife (Belinda)
Coins (Dr. Jack)

Act I, Scene 3—Grist Mill

On Stage
Fiddle and bow (Hector McGuffey)
Fiddle case

Act II, Scene 1—Kitchen

On Stage
Needlepoint frame
Wood box
Wood stove

Shelves (right)
Sink, with hand pump (cupboard underneath)
Table

Chairs (3)
Kerosene lamp
Stool
Horsehair sofa
  Blanket (on sofa)
Roller towel (over sink)
Wall calendar, with likeness of
  Madonna on it
Spinning wheel
Small table
Shotgun (over door, upstage)
Bible
Pail, with nails in it (under sink)
Bag of popcorn } (in pantry)
Dish of butter

Frying pan } (on stove)
Tin, pan cover
Bowl (on shelves, right)
Salt cellar (on shelves, right)
Jug of liquor } (in pantry)
Glasses (2)
Off Left
Nightgown (Maggie)
Off Upstage
Book of sign language } (Dr. Jack)
Alphabet cards
Personal
Pipe (McDonald)

Act II, Scene 2—Kitchen

On Stage
Water glass (on sink)
Account book (in drawer of table, center)
Pails (2), with feed for pigs

Off Upstage
Floppy, straw hat } (Maggie)
Bunch of carrots
Personal
Coins (Dr. Jack)

Act II, Scene 3—Bedroom

On Stage
Spool bed
  Patch-work quilt
Rocking chair
Bureau, on it:
  Kerosene lamp
  Vase of flowers
  Glass, for medicine
  Spoon
Off Left
Cup of broth (Maggie)

Act II, Scene 4—Kitchen

On Stage
Cradle
Account book
Work basket, in it:
  Pair of baby mittens
  Baby cap
  Balls of wool
Broom (in pantry)
Pipe (McDoinald, on shelves, right)
Glasses (2, on sink)
Pail of nails (by sink)
Copy books (2, on shelves, right)
Off Left
Life-size baby doll (Belinda)
Off Upstage
Doctor's bag (Dr. Jack)
  Bottle of Scotch whiskey
Piece of meat (McDonald)

Act III, Scene 1—Kitchen

On Stage
Saucepan ⎫
  Baby's bottles ⎬ (on stove)
Kettle ⎪
Tea pot ⎭
Tray, (in pantry), on it:
  Cups (3)
  Saucers (3)
  Spoons (3)
  Sugar bowl
  Cream pitcher
Cake ⎫
Cake knife ⎬ (in pantry)
Plates (3) ⎭
Cup, saucer and plate, for Stella (in pantry)

Off Upstage
Paper bag, with baby sweater (Stella)
Fur coat and cap (Dr. Jack)
Fur coat (Rev. Tidmarsh)
Fur coats (2, Mrs. Lutz and Mrs. McKee)
Coat and cap (Locky)
Coat (Stella)
Off Left
Baby blanket (Belinda)
Personal
Pad and pencil ⎫
Map ⎬ (Dr. Jack)
Wristwatch ⎭
List, on piece of paper (Mrs. Lutz)
Pince-nez (Rev. Tidmarsh)

Act III, Scene 2—Kitchen

On Stage
Churn of buttermilk
Bucket
Wooden bowl, with butter in it
Cake (in pantry)
Box of shotgun shells (on shelves, right)

Overshoes ⎫
Cap ⎬
Mackinaw ⎬ (Belinda)
Mittens ⎭
Coat (Stella, on sofa)

Act III, Scene 3—Courtroom

On Stage
Chairs (12)
Desk
Platform

Picture of Queen Victoria
Personal
Robes and wig (Judge)
Handkerchief (Dr. Jack)

SOUND EFFECTS

Act I, Scene 2

Chicken cackling   Cow moo-ing
Bird singing

Act II, Scene 3

"Shivaree" sounds—music, laughter and voices

Act II, Scene 4

Roll of thunder

Act III, Scene 2

Firing of shotgun

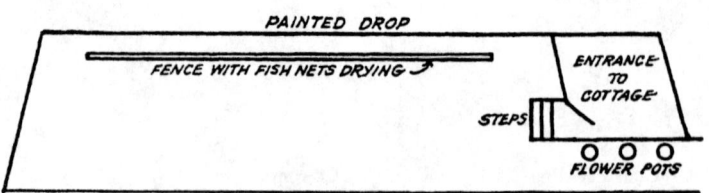

VILLAGE STREET – Act I, Scene 1

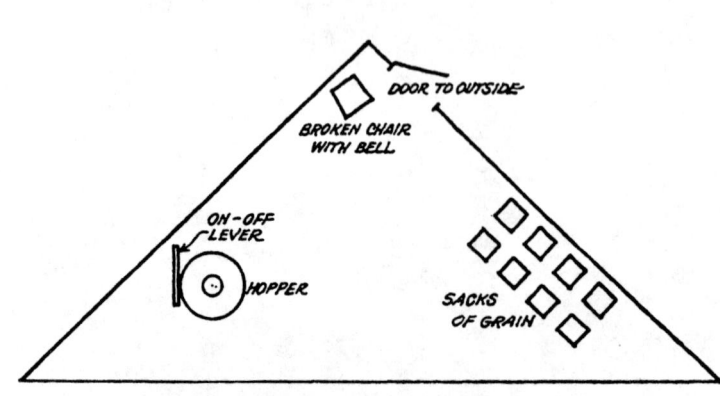

GRIST MILL – Act I, Scenes 2 & 3

SCENE DESIGNS
"JOHNNY BELINDA"

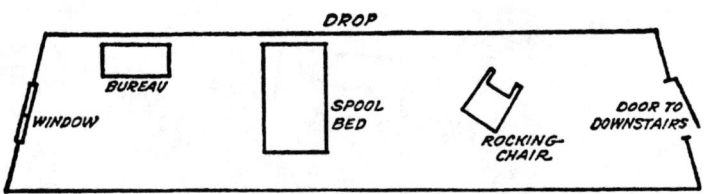

BEDROOM — Act II, Scene 3

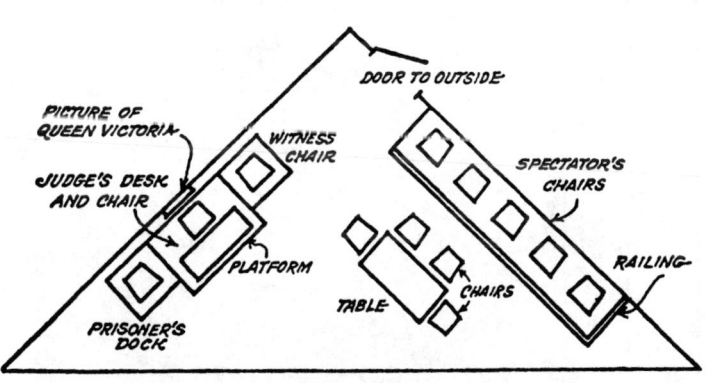

COURT ROOM — Act III, Scene 3

SCENE DESIGNS
"JOHNNY BELINDA"

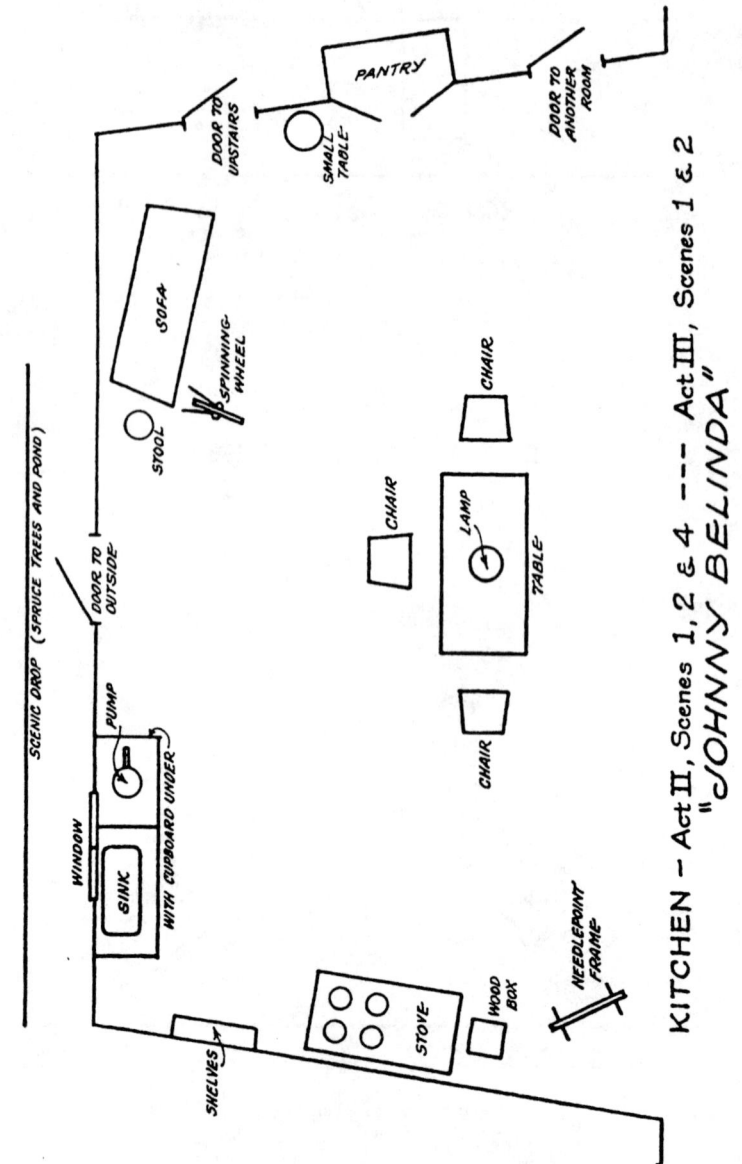

KITCHEN — Act II, Scenes 1, 2 & 4 --- Act III, Scenes 1 & 2
"JOHNNY BELINDA"

LIST OF DEAF MUTE SIGNS USED IN "JOHNNY BELINDA"

Page No.	Interpretation
23	Fish
	Chicken
24	Bird Cow Milking—Horns Write Talk Pleased I am pleased to meet you. I shall see you again soon. Goodby
29	I can talk.
35	Thank you. Man Gentleman
36	Woman Father Mother Grandfather Ancestors
38	Good night—Good day Morning, noon, afternoon, evening Daughter Lessons We must get to work. A B C D. (*Signed separately.*)
44	Why is my father angry? Very tired. Who will do my work? Your father will do it.

Page No.	Interpretation

44
- My father is angry.
- No, he is not angry. He was worried. He has lots of worries. He wants to ask your forgiveness. Do you forgive him?
- You taught me.
- I taught you what?

45
- Forgive us our trespasses as we forgive those who trespass against us.

- Try it. It will do you good.

- What is going on out there?
- What is going on outside? That's a party.
- I have never been to a party.
- You haven't had much fun. You have been very lonely. But you won't be lonely any more.
- You are to become a mother.

46
- Mother?

- Yes. You.
- I want a boy.
- Why not a girl?
- No. A boy.
- All right. We shall hope for a boy.

- You forgot the T.
- Would you be wantin' anything?
- What has he got?
- He's got a cow?
- Is it dead?
- I'm laughing at you.

48
- What would you be likin'?
- Anything else?
- B—A—K—E
- Hearing?
- Fine! Nothing wrong with his hearing, thank heaven!
- Perfect
- Pleasure

50
- Man
- Woman
- Baby
- Who is the most beautiful girl in the world?

	Interpretation

	Is everything all right?
	What did you tell my father?
	I was telling him what a fine girl you are, and how pleased I am with the progress you are making with your lessons.

	Lightning
53	Yes—and thunder too.
	I love thunder storms.
	Oh, you love thunder storms, do you?
	I don't.
	Fire
	Music
	Your homework

	What's This?
	Some work
	I like signs
	Coming through the Rye for me.
	I know it.
	Oh, you know it, do you? Well, let me see.
	If a body meets a body
	Coming through the Rye
54	If a body kiss a body
	Need a body cry?
	Every Lassie has her Laddie
	Not one they say have I
	Yet all the boys they smile at me
	Coming through the Rye.
	I am not afraid.
	I want to try some oral work.
	Speaking

	Talking
	Two syllables—John-ny.
55	
	Your father is hurt—the lightning.
	Dead

	Our Father, who art in Heaven,
	Hallowed be Thy name.
	Thy Kingdom Come
56	Thy will be done
	on Earth as it is in Heaven.
	Give us this day our daily bread
	and forgive us our trespasses

Page No.   *Interpretation*

56
> as we forgive those who trespass against us.
> Lead us not into temptation
> But deliver us from evil.
> For Thine is the Kingdom
> and the power
> and the glory forever.
> Amen.
>
> Good night, father.

57
> Beautiful
> Did you make it?
> I like this very much.
> I can't stay.
> I haven't much time.
> A few minutes.
> I shall send for you.

58
> I'm going away. I must catch a train in forty minutes.
> Why?
> Because I must make some money.
> Where are you going?
> Long travel. On the boat. On the train. A thousand miles. Montreal.
> When will you come back?
> I'll be back for Christmas.
> Be careful.
> I shall die if harm comes to you.
> I love you.
> What does marriage mean to you?
>
> I—have—seen—a young man—and a young woman—come smiling from—the church—and drive away—and live together—under one roof—and children come—and laughter—but always they—are together—in joy— in happiness—in work—and play—until they—are old. That is marriage to me.
> We'll have a Christmas tree and presents for you and your mother.
> Don't forget me.
> I can't forget you. You are in my mind and my heart always. Goodbye, dear.

Page No.	Interpretation
59	I am pleased to meet you all.
60	Seeing you all here gives me great pleasure.
67	In my endless silence—life was meaningless—until he came. I fed him—I kept him warm—I could not sleep—if he fell ill —— And when he smiled—my heart was filled with song —— I love him better than my life.
68	He hurt me. I was afraid he would hurt my child. You are free.
69	I—love—my—baby!

NEW PLAYS

★ **SHEL'S SHORTS by Shel Silverstein.** Lauded poet, songwriter and author of children's books, the incomparable Shel Silverstein's short plays are deeply infused with the same wicked sense of humor that made him famous. "…[a] childlike honesty and twisted sense of humor." –*Boston Herald.* "…terse dialogue and an absurdity laced with a tang of dread give [*Shel's Shorts*] more than a trace of Samuel Beckett's comic existentialism." –*Boston Phoenix.* [flexible casting] ISBN: 0-8222-1897-6

★ **AN ADULT EVENING OF SHEL SILVERSTEIN by Shel Silverstein.** Welcome to the darkly comic world of Shel Silverstein, a world where nothing is as it seems and where the most innocent conversation can turn menacing in an instant. These ten imaginative plays vary widely in content, but the style is unmistakable. "…[*An Adult Evening*] shows off Silverstein's virtuosic gift for wordplay…[and] sends the audience out…with a clear appreciation of human nature as perverse and laughable." –*NY Times.* [flexible casting] ISBN: 0-8222-1873-9

★ **WHERE'S MY MONEY? by John Patrick Shanley.** A caustic and sardonic vivisection of the institution of marriage, laced with the author's inimitable razor-sharp wit. "…Shanley's gift for acid-laced one-liners and emotionally tumescent exchanges is certainly potent…" –*Variety.* "…lively, smart, occasionally scary and rich in reverse wisdom." –*NY Times.* [3M, 3W] ISBN: 0-8222-1865-8

★ **A FEW STOUT INDIVIDUALS by John Guare.** A wonderfully screwy comedy-drama that figures Ulysses S. Grant in the throes of writing his memoirs, surrounded by a cast of fantastical characters, including the Emperor and Empress of Japan, the opera star Adelina Patti and Mark Twain. "Guare's smarts, passion and creativity skyrocket to awesome heights…" –*Star Ledger.* "…precisely the kind of good new play that you might call an everyday miracle…every minute of it is fresh and newly alive…" –*Village Voice.* [10M, 3W] ISBN: 0-8222-1907-7

★ **BREATH, BOOM by Kia Corthron.** A look at fourteen years in the life of Prix, a Bronx native, from her ruthless girl-gang leadership at sixteen through her coming to maturity at thirty. "…vivid world, believable and eye-opening, a place worthy of a dramatic visit, where no one would want to live but many have to." –*NY Times.* "…rich with humor, terse vernacular strength and gritty detail…" –*Variety.* [1M, 9W] ISBN: 0-8222-1849-6

★ **THE LATE HENRY MOSS by Sam Shepard.** Two antagonistic brothers, Ray and Earl, are brought together after their father, Henry Moss, is found dead in his seedy New Mexico home in this classic Shepard tale. "…His singular gift has been for building mysteries out of the ordinary ingredients of American family life…" –*NY Times.* "…rich moments …Shepard finds gold." –*LA Times.* [7M, 1W] ISBN: 0-8222-1858-5

★ **THE CARPETBAGGER'S CHILDREN by Horton Foote.** One family's history spanning from the Civil War to WWII is recounted by three sisters in evocative, intertwining monologues. "…bittersweet music—[a] rhapsody of ambivalence…in its modest, garrulous way…theatrically daring." –*The New Yorker.* [3W] ISBN: 0-8222-1843-7

★ **THE NINA VARIATIONS by Steven Dietz.** In this funny, fierce and heartbreaking homage to *The Seagull*, Dietz puts Chekhov's star-crossed lovers in a room and doesn't let them out. "A perfect little jewel of a play…" –*Shepherdstown Chronicle.* "…a delightful revelation of a writer at play; and also an odd, haunting, moving theater piece of lingering beauty." –*Eastside Journal (Seattle).* [1M, 1W (flexible casting)] ISBN: 0-8222-1891-7

DRAMATISTS PLAY SERVICE, INC.
440 Park Avenue South, New York, NY 10016 212-683-8960 Fax 212-213-1539
postmaster@dramatists.com   www.dramatists.com

NEW PLAYS

★ **BE AGGRESSIVE by Annie Weisman.** Vista Del Sol is paradise, sandy beaches, avocado-lined streets. But for seventeen-year-old cheerleader Laura, everything changes when her mother is killed in a car crash, and she embarks on a journey to the Spirit Institute of the South where she can learn "cheer" with Bible belt intensity. "...filled with lingual gymnastics...stylized rapid-fire dialogue..." –*Variety*. "...a new, exciting, and unique voice in the American theatre..." –*BackStage West*. [1M, 4W, extras] ISBN: 0-8222-1894-1

★ **FOUR by Christopher Shinn.** Four people struggle desperately to connect in this quiet, sophisticated, moving drama. "...smart, broken-hearted...Mr. Shinn has a precocious and forgiving sense of how power shifts in the game of sexual pursuit...He promises to be a playwright to reckon with..." –*NY Times*. "A voice emerges from an American place. It's got humor, sadness and a fresh and touching rhythm that tell of the loneliness and secrets of life...[a] poetic, haunting play." –*NY Post*. [3M, 1W] ISBN: 0-8222-1850-X

★ **WONDER OF THE WORLD by David Lindsay-Abaire.** A madcap picaresque involving Niagara Falls, a lonely tour-boat captain, a pair of bickering private detectives and a husband's dirty little secret. "Exceedingly whimsical and playfully wicked. Winning and genial. A top-drawer production." –*NY Times*. "Full frontal lunacy is on display. A most assuredly fresh and hilarious tragicomedy of marital discord run amok...absolutely hysterical..." –*Variety*. [3M, 4W (doubling)] ISBN: 0-8222-1863-1

★ **QED by Peter Parnell.** Nobel Prize-winning physicist and all-around genius Richard Feynman holds forth with captivating wit and wisdom in this fascinating biographical play that originally starred Alan Alda. "QED is a seductive mix of science, human affections, moral courage, and comic eccentricity. It reflects on, among other things, death, the absence of God, travel to an unexplored country, the pleasures of drumming, and the need to know and understand." –*NY Magazine*. "Its rhythms correspond to the way that people—even geniuses—approach and avoid highly emotional issues, and it portrays Feynman with affection and awe." –*The New Yorker*. [1M, 1W] ISBN: 0-8222-1924-7

★ **UNWRAP YOUR CANDY by Doug Wright.** Alternately chilling and hilarious, this deliciously macabre collection of four bedtime tales for adults is guaranteed to keep you awake for nights on end. "Engaging and intellectually satisfying...a treat to watch." –*NY Times*. "Fiendishly clever. Mordantly funny and chilling. Doug Wright teases, freezes and zaps us." –*Village Voice*. "Four bite-size plays that bite back." –*Variety*. [flexible casting] ISBN: 0-8222-1871-2

★ **FURTHER THAN THE FURTHEST THING by Zinnie Harris.** On a remote island in the middle of the Atlantic secrets are buried. When the outside world comes calling, the islanders find their world blown apart from the inside as well as beyond. "Harris winningly produces an intimate and poetic, as well as political, family saga." –*Independent (London)*. "Harris' enthralling adventure of a play marks a departure from stale, well-furrowed theatrical terrain." –*Evening Standard (London)*. [3M, 2W] ISBN: 0-8222-1874-7

★ **THE DESIGNATED MOURNER by Wallace Shawn.** The story of three people living in a country where what sort of books people like to read and how they choose to amuse themselves becomes both firmly personal and unexpectedly entangled with questions of survival. "This is a playwright who does not just tell you what it is like to be arrested at night by goons or to fall morally apart and become an aimless yet weirdly contented ghost yourself. He has the originality to make you feel it." –*Times (London)*. "A fascinating play with beautiful passages of writing..." –*Variety*. [2M, 1W] ISBN: 0-8222-1848-8

DRAMATISTS PLAY SERVICE, INC.
440 Park Avenue South, New York, NY 10016 212-683-8960 Fax 212-213-1539
postmaster@dramatists.com www.dramatists.com

NEW PLAYS

★ **MONTHS ON END by Craig Pospisil.** In comic scenes, one for each month of the year, we follow the intertwined worlds of a circle of friends and family whose lives are poised between happiness and heartbreak. "...a triumph...these twelve vignettes all form crucial pieces in the eternal puzzle known as human relationships, an area in which the playwright displays an assured knowledge that spans deep sorrow to unbounded happiness." –*Ann Arbor News.* "...rings with emotional truth, humor...[an] endearing contemplation on love...entertaining and satisfying." –*Oakland Press.* [5M, 5W] ISBN: 0-8222-1892-5

★ **GOOD THING by Jessica Goldberg.** Brings us into the households of John and Nancy Roy, forty-something high-school guidance counselors whose marriage has been increasingly on the rocks and Dean and Mary, recent graduates struggling to make their way in life. "...a blend of gritty social drama, poetic humor and unsubtle existential contemplation..." –*Variety.* [3M, 3W] ISBN: 0-8222-1869-0

★ **THE DEAD EYE BOY by Angus MacLachlan.** Having fallen in love at their Narcotics Anonymous meeting, Billy and Shirley-Diane are striving to overcome the past together. But their relationship is complicated by the presence of Sorin, Shirley-Diane's fourteen-year-old son, a damaged reminder of her dark past. "...a grim, insightful portrait of an unmoored family..." –*NY Times.* "MacLachlan's play isn't for the squeamish, but then, tragic stories delivered at such an unrelenting fever pitch rarely are." –*Variety.* [1M, 1W, 1 boy] ISBN: 0-8222-1844-6

★ **[SIC] by Melissa James Gibson.** In adjacent apartments three young, ambitious neighbors come together to discuss, flirt, argue, share their dreams and plan their futures with unequal degrees of deep hopefulness and abject despair. "A work...concerned with the sound and power of language..." –*NY Times.* "...a wonderfully original take on urban friendship and the comedy of manners—a *Design for Living* for our times..." –*NY Observer.* [3M, 2W] ISBN: 0-8222-1872-0

★ **LOOKING FOR NORMAL by Jane Anderson.** Roy and Irma's twenty-five-year marriage is thrown into turmoil when Roy confesses that he is actually a woman trapped in a man's body, forcing the couple to wrestle with the meaning of their marriage and the delicate dynamics of family. "Jane Anderson's bittersweet transgender domestic comedy-drama ...is thoughtful and touching and full of wit and wisdom. A real audience pleaser." –*Hollywood Reporter.* [5M, 4W] ISBN: 0-8222-1857-7

★ **ENDPAPERS by Thomas McCormack.** The regal Joshua Maynard, the old and ailing head of a mid-sized, family-owned book-publishing house in New York City, must name a successor. One faction in the house backs a smart, "pragmatic" manager, the other faction a smart, "sensitive" editor and both factions fear what the other's man could do to this house—and to them. "If Kaufman and Hart had undertaken a comedy about the publishing business, they might have written *Endpapers*...a breathlessly fast, funny, and thoughtful comedy ...keeps you amused, guessing, and often surprised...profound in its empathy for the paradoxes of human nature." –*NY Magazine.* [7M, 4W] ISBN: 0-8222-1908-5

★ **THE PAVILION by Craig Wright.** By turns poetic and comic, romantic and philosophical, this play asks old lovers to face the consequences of difficult choices made long ago. "The script's greatest strength lies in the genuineness of its feeling." –*Houston Chronicle.* "Wright's perceptive, gently witty writing makes this familiar situation fresh and thoroughly involving." –*Philadelphia Inquirer.* [2M, 1W (flexible casting)] ISBN: 0-8222-1898-4

DRAMATISTS PLAY SERVICE, INC.
440 Park Avenue South, New York, NY 10016 212-683-8960 Fax 212-213-1539
postmaster@dramatists.com www.dramatists.com